GOD'S STORY, OUR STORY

EXPLORING CHRISTIAN FAITH AND LIFE

MICHELE HERSHBERGER

Herald Press

Harrisonburg, Virginia
Waterloo, Ontario

Library of Congress Catalog-In-Publication Data
Hershberger, Michele, 1960-
  God's story, our story : exploring Christian faith and life / by Michele Hershberger.
-- Revision edition
    pages cm.
  ISBN 978-0-8361-9693-1 (pbk. : alk. paper) 1. Mennonites--Doctrines.
2. Initiation rites--Religious aspects--Mennonites. 3. Baptism and church member-
ship. I. Title.
  BX8121.3.H47 2013
  230'.97--dc23

                                        2013011428

GOD'S STORY, OUR STORY
by Michele Hershberger
Copyright © 2003, 2013 by Herald Press, Harrisonburg, VA 22802
            Published simultaneously in Canada by Herald Press,
            Waterloo, ON N2L 6H7
Library of Congress number 2013011428
International Standard Book Number 978-0-8361-9693-1
Printed in the United States of America
Cover and interior design by Merrill R. Miller

18 17 16 15 14 13   10 9 8 7 6 5 4 3 2 1

To order or request information, please call 1-800-245-7894 in the U.S.
or 1-800-631-6535 in Canada. Or visit www.heraldpress.com.

Herald Press
www.heraldpress.com

Table of Contents

Author's Acknowledgments

God's Story, Our Story has enjoyed 10 years of service as a guide on the journey toward baptism. So when approached about updating the book to make it more current, I was delighted. I want to thank everyone who reviewed and offered feedback on the original *God's Story, Our Story* and also everyone who gave helpful critique in preparation for this edition. I especially want to thank Mary Ann Weber for collecting new stories, and Andrea Peters, whose young eyes helped me see the text in a new way.

It is my sincere hope and prayer that those who use it will grow in their Christian faith. God's story is as relevant today as it was so many years ago. We are invited to join in this story and make it our own, which opens the door for us to be transformed into the image of Christ and be vessels of Christ's love to the world.

Writing this new baptismal resource has been an intense challenge for me. But there are many who lightened up the load and made it a joyful experience. First, I want to thank the group who first conceived of the project, then critiqued the draft manuscript: Marlene Kropf (the group's chair), Palmer Becker, Ruth Boehm, Shirley Brubaker Yoder, Byron Rempel-Burkholder, Steve Ropp, Regina Shands Stoltzfus, Dale Shenk, Karl Steffy, Bob Yoder, and April Yamasaki. Several others added their feedback on the manuscript: Gary Blosser, Anne Campion, Edwin Epp, Omar Martin, Henry Paetkau, Gabrielle Plenert, and Elsie Rempel.

A second group met with me every week to discuss the chapters. Words can't begin to express my gratitude for Mike Mendez, Rosella Wedel, Josh Piper, Luke Hartman, and Tara Hershberger. These dear friends carried me through and spoke God's word to me on those Saturday mornings. This book is theirs in so many ways. Thanks also to Mary Simmering and Heidi Boese, for reading the manuscript and jumping into the conversation midstream.

The junior high Sunday school class at Hesston Mennonite Church helped me field test this material and they told me what didn't work, what really did work, and why. They also share in the writing of this book; their passion for God gives me such hope for the future.

My editor, Byron Rempel-Burkholder, engaged himself in ways that went far beyond the call of duty. He reworked my manuscript tirelessly. He saw his work, as I do, as a ministry. My deep thanks to him.

I am also deeply indebted to my colleague and mentor, Marion Bontrager. In many ways, Marion helped me put the story together, and in that sense, this is his book, too.

Finally, I thank my husband, Del, and three children for putting up with me during this long process. Their love and support through the long hours and sleepless nights means so much to me.
—*Michele Hershberger*

Pull Up a Chair...

If I had just one chance to talk to you about faith, to discuss who God is and why Jesus came, what would I say? If I had a chance, just one chance, to say whatever I thought would help you begin to know Jesus, what words would I use?

We have this time—now—to talk about what matters in life. It is a conversation of greatest importance, a journey inside of you and toward God. It is also a journey that eventually leads out to others, changing your whole life.

Some people call it faith exploration. Others see it as that time when you ask the big questions of life. For many, this journey will lead to baptism in a local congregation. I see it as an encounter with the Story about God working in the world, and a time to figure out what we choose to do with that story.

The quest

There's nothing wrong with the big questions. They're important, and we'll deal with some in this book. Everyone wants to know what the meaning of life is, and how to find joy. It's also apparent that something is incredibly wrong with the world today. What causes this wrongness? What is the problem?

Especially in North America, we have to wonder why, given all our material wealth, many are not happy. The people who have the most in our societies—celebrities—are four times more likely to commit suicide than the average person. The ones who have it all—sports stars, Hollywood entertainers, and musicians—live an average of only 56 years, compared to the average life span of around 72.

What's wrong with this picture? The common approach to life—live for yourself, grab all the gusto you can, look out for number one—doesn't seem to work in the long run, and deep down inside, we know that. But what does work? What will bring us true joy?

The quest continues

My list of my big questions keeps growing. Since the first printing of this book 10 years ago, a lot has happened. Several researchers have made significant contributions to our understanding of North American youth and their interaction with faith.

Christian Smith and Melinda Lundquist Denton wrote the book *Soul Searching*, which speaks of a trend among Christians, both youth and adults, to worship a moralistic, therapeutic, deistic god that only slightly resembles the God of the Bible. Are we part of that trend? It's interesting that one of the authors' solutions to the problem is that we drench ourselves in the stories of the Bible, not just in the stories we like or find easy to understand, but all the stories. We are not to skip the stories that are difficult to understand or flinch at the mysteries that won't go away. God is more than a butler that we can call on when we get into trouble. God is more than a God who wants us to share and be polite. Are we diving into the biblical story enough to hear the real God?

Researcher Chap Clark identifies another trend in his book *Hurt*. More youth than ever are feeling abandoned by the adults in their lives. Abandonment can come in the form of adults rejecting youth, expecting too much from them, or simply not being there when youth need them. Many youth are hurting. At a recent Mennonite Church USA youth convention, more than 3,000 youth and adults wrote about their pain on small pieces of paper and turned them in: the pain of addictions, broken relationships, shame, and fear. We prayed over their words and wondered why there was so much pain. Are we trying to fit God into an image that looks suspiciously close . . . to us? And does that effort have any connection with all the pain we're feeling?

A story of joy

One of my dearest friends is a woman who lives in a big city and works at a halfway house for kids in trouble with the law. She doesn't make much money—hardly any—and the kids often drive her nuts. Her jobs range from talking to senators about criminal justice to mopping floors. And she beams. She gets tired sometimes, and downright worried about her finances, but even when she has mopped one too many floors—she beams. She radiates.

Does that mean that true happiness comes when you work for some social service agency? Or is there something more to it? I don't have all the answers. But I am convinced that there is a Source from which the most important answers flow. I believe it's God, the God we can really know through Jesus Christ. How do I know this? Well, scientifically, I can't prove it. It's not something I can figure out with logic alone. But I know. I have encountered God and Jesus through the Story, the story of God as written in the Bible. I've also encountered God and Jesus through relationships with my church family, through my experiences, and through the whispering of the Spirit in my life. Along with millions of others throughout history, I have said yes to the Story and have accepted it as my own.

This book is a journey into the Story. We will begin with the biblical narrative, not with black and white truth statements or even the big life questions. As we engage the Story, big life questions will pop up. In fact, the Story will even help us shape those questions.

Talking it through

This book is also a conversation among several participants: you, me, *other people whom I'll introduce shortly*—and most of all, with the Bible itself. We'll be honest about our inability to hear this last partner completely. No one can be completely objective about the Bible. Everyone sees it through his or her own "glasses" of culture and experience, and we'll talk about that, too. Nevertheless, the Bible will be our most important conversation partner.

Another conversation partner will be the church, both the Anabaptist/Mennonite branch, and the larger, older, worldwide church. Along with the Bible and the church, history and experience will have a few words to say as well.

I've invited some of my friends—real people—to join in the conversation on the following pages. We'll talk in a way that will help us keep each other honest, but also have a little fun along the way. Let these friends introduce themselves:

Tara. I'm 15 and in high school. We have moved around a lot and that has been a hard, but maybe a good thing in my life. I was baptized when I was pretty young—nine—and I wonder if I really knew what I was doing. But I do know this: Something happened. And it was good. It was real. But now I have a lot of questions, and really want to take my faith to the next level.

Mike. I am 20, and I think a lot about this faith stuff. When I was in high school, I had people come up to me and tell me that if I would die tonight I would go to hell, and I don't know . . .

something turned me off about that. I was kind of an atheist after that. I went to university and really struggled with grades, drank a lot, and dropped out of classes. I did take a Bible course at this Mennonite college, and that was really great. I've just learned so much, and I want to learn more.

Rosella. I have been a Christian for a long time. I'm 83 years old, you know. My husband died several years ago and for a while I didn't know if I was going to make it. But God helped me out through my friends, my pastor, and my family. I thought, how could I repay all that kindness? So I joined the Caring Connection. My main ministry is to head up the food pantry. You would not believe the needs of people. Many times it is not just food; they need warmth and kindness.

Luke. I'm 33 and a college teacher and coach. When I was seven days old, my parents adopted me as an interracial child into an all-white family. I was a preacher's kid. It was a good childhood, but in many ways I just accepted the party line. And now here I am, a young adult, and I'm finding I have a lot of questions. That's kind of unsettling.

Josh. I'm 18 years old. My parents always raised me with a good Christian background, and I've always gone to church. Just recently, God has become more real to me, and the problems of the world have also become more real to me.

Mary. I'm 13, the youngest in the group, but hey, I've got some of the best questions. I enjoy playing softball and I love the great outdoors. I write a lot of poetry, too.

Join us

As we discuss our faith and try to live it out, we invite you to join us in the conversation. We also invite you to do something really important. We invite you to enter the Story—this unfolding drama of God's work in the world and in your life. You can know about it and explain it and be able to analyze it from several different viewpoints. But the real satisfaction comes in accepting the Story as your own. Knowing *about* Jesus is not the same as knowing Jesus, following him, and having a life-changing, everyday relationship with one who lived, died, rose again, and still lives—for you.

That's what this book is about. So pull up a chair. Have some brownies. Let's talk.

So pull up a chair.

Have some brownies.

Let's talk.

Topics in chapter 1

- **God sets the stage—a good creation**
- **People in God's image**
- **God—far off and yet close up**
- **Humanity's problem: sin**
- **God's judgment and God's grace**

Story line:
Creation
Adam and Eve
Tower of Babel

1. Beginnings

The Bible makes a big deal about God as Creator of the world. It opens with the Divine Being calling the world into being, and doing it with intention and love (Genesis 1, 2). What a far cry from what you get in the science classroom, where the world seems to come together impersonally and by chance. It's also quite different from other ancient creation stories where the gods create the world by violence. We Christians take by faith that God spoke the word and the world came into being. We believe God made a beautiful, perfect creation.

"God saw everything that he had made, and indeed, it was very good" (Gen 1:31).

Some ancient religions would have called nature divine—part of God—while others saw the physical world as corrupt and not worth saving. But the ancient followers of the God of the Bible understood creation, including human beings, as something that has value. If that's true, then it changes how we treat our bodies and all of nature. We have a responsibility to care for what God has called good. But our bodies aren't God, just like the mighty sequoia trees are not God. Nature—from mountains to trees to our bodies—is not to be worshiped. That's why the Bible also makes a big deal about the sin of idolatry (see Exod 20:4-6; also page 41).

How is your life different if you choose to see all of God's creation as good, including your own self? How does it affect how you treat others?

Humans are made in God's image. Our bodies are good because God created nature and the physical world this way. But humans are also special because they—both males and females—have been created in God's image (Gen 1:26-27). We can think and feel in ways that animals can't. Like God, we have free will. Like God, we are spiritual beings. God gives us the responsibility to "have dominion" and care for the earth.

God—far off and close up. The book of Genesis gives us two creation stories that show us two different pictures of God. In Genesis 1, we see God as all-powerful, mighty, and high above us. God speaks the word, and worlds are created. This shows God's transcendence— above us, beyond us, too mysterious for us to know, too awesome for us to do anything but worship.

What does it mean to be made in the image of God?

Mike: It means I'm glad to be alive.

Tara: God doesn't make junk.

Rosella: Each one of us is unique, special, beautiful because of who we are in God.

Mike: But why didn't God just make us perfect? Why did God give us the ability to screw up?

Luke: I like the idea of choice, even though it hasn't always served me well.

Josh: Freedom of choice makes us human. God wants people who will be faithful because they choose that.

Rosella: Is it possible to be made in the image of God and not have that choice?

Luke: Sometimes it bothers me when people say, "sinful like human nature." We make choices that can either help others become more human, or dehumanize them. To be truly human is to love like God, to be like Jesus.

Tara: I heard that "have dominion over" means men having dominion over women. I think that's a crock. Male and female are created in God's image, thank you very much.

Luke: Is God a male? I don't think God is. Just like God is not white or black. God is beyond all that.

Then in Genesis 2, we see God in another way—God as one who is close and relational. God walks on the earth and gently bends down to form Adam's body from the earth. These two images complement each other. We need both the high God and the personal God (Isa 6:1-11). One image of God, one creation story, can't contain all there is. God is both close-up and personal, far off and beyond knowing.

Which part of God are you more comfortable with—the close-up and personal God or the all-powerful, mysterious God?

Tara: God is merciful, but must be feared. You read all these Bible stories where they do one thing wrong, then God sends the prophet to go tell them they're going to die along with their children. Ugh.

Mike: A lot of people have this image of God with the long white hair and sitting up on this golden throne with a magic hand that does stuff. God is more . . . what's the word . . . spirit.

Josh: I love the idea that God is all-powerful but still wants to be with us on a personal level. It's one of those things that we can't fathom but it's how it is because God is God.

Mike: God is like the number you can't possibly count to.

Creation of Adam —Michelangelo

God is a mystery . . . yet we know God through Jesus. The two creation stories give us the first paradox about God—far off and unknowable, and yet close-up and personal. Jesus continued the paradox. Christians believe he was completely God, including all the awesome glory that we can't begin to comprehend. Yet, all that glory became a human baby. The New Testament writer John tells how the Word "became flesh"—a person just like you and me (John 1:14). What an incredible way to begin to know and understand what is absolutely beyond our understanding! Jesus walked on the earth, feeling pain and hunger, struggling with the temptation to sin, laughing at jokes until his sides split. The unknowable became knowable through Jesus. What a gift to us!

Christians talk about God being omnipresent (everywhere), omniscient (knows everything), and omnipotent (all powerful). Yet those terms alone don't describe God fully. In Jesus, the all-powerful One came to earth and allowed himself to be rejected, cursed, beaten, and eventually crucified. That combination of omnipotence and obedient love, even to the point of death, is found in no other religion (1 John 4:8–10). The Almighty One, who wouldn't have to want us, who didn't have to come to earth to be with us, goes to great lengths to have a relationship with us.

What does it mean to have a relationship with God? How is it more than just saying yes to a set of statements about God?

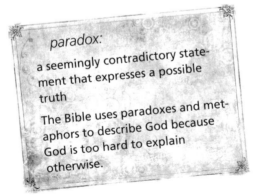

paradox: a seemingly contradictory state-ment that expresses a possible truth

The Bible uses paradoxes and met-aphors to describe God because God is too hard to explain otherwise.

What does God look like?

The Bible uses dozens of metaphors—word images—to try to tell us what God is like. Three of them, among many, are:

- God as a mother hen (Luke 13:34)

- God as a warrior (Ps 3; see page 36)

- God as a shepherd (Ps 23; Ps 80:1)

But God can't be summed up in any of those metaphors. Every time we use a metaphor for God we risk putting God in a box (see Isa 40:18-31; Rom 11:33-36). In Genesis 3:8, for example, God is pictured as "walking" through the Garden of Eden. Do we understand God literally to have feet, or is the writer using such language to help us understand something that is beyond explanation?

Living it out

Beginnings: As I grew in faith I discovered that God became real to me through beginnings. Beginning something new is exciting, whether we are starting a new book or learning a new song, and we know that God is a part of beginnings because he created the world that we live in. We hear about this in the story of creation in the book of Genesis, and also in John 1:1, which says "In the beginning was the Word, and the Word was with God." Something that made sense to me when I began to explore faith was the idea that God spoke the world into being. The eternal word of God seems distant and mysterious, while the act of speaking is personal and close. This paradox shows us that God is very different than us, but also just like us. Although this looks contradictory to our limited human perspectives, we trust that it makes sense to God who sees how all of creation fits together. —*Max Kennel, Waterloo, Ontario*

God wants relationship with humans. One 17th century summary of Christian faith, the Westminster Longer Catechism, states that our purpose in life is to "glorify God and to enjoy him forever." From the Bible's opening, it is clear that God also wants to enjoy us! In the creation stories we can see that longing for relationship. The Lord walked in the garden, talking with Adam and Eve. And God gave them choice, whether or not to refrain from eating the forbidden fruit of the Tree of Knowledge and the Tree of Life (Gen 2, 3). Even after they sinned, God sought them out, calling their names (Gen 3:9), and caring for them. In a nutshell, that's what the rest of the Story is about. It's a beautiful tale of the loving Creator seeking out the beloved creation—you and me—to communicate one thing . . . I love you. But first . . .

Things fall apart—the problem of sin

In the biblical story, humans soon make choices that are wrong and against God's will. And with that choice comes the problem that is at the center of the Story's development: sin. The Bible starts off with four stories in close succession that show different angles of the human problem of sin. We see four major relationships broken: our relationship with God, our relationship with our inner selves, our relationship with each other, and our relationship with the physical world. We also see how sin tends to get more complicated, snowballing into increasingly bad situations.

Story 1. Trying to be like God. In the first story, Adam and Eve sin by wanting to be like God. The serpent contradicts God's instructions not to eat the fruit from the Tree of the Knowledge of Good and Evil. Eating the fruit, it says, will make them "like God" (Gen 3:5). Adam and Eve are led to believe that they will become "wise" (Gen 3:6). In some ways, all sin is trying to be like God. When one person kills

Mosaic from Cathedral of Monreale, 13th Century

Mary: Now I'm confused. I thought we were supposed to try to be like God.

Michele: We are called to be godly people, growing up to be more and more like Christ. But we sin when we act as if we're in control of the world—being proud, taking into our hands what really belongs to God.

Rosella: Isn't it funny that Jesus, even though he was God, humbled himself to become human? He let go of all the advantages of being God—while the rest of us try to grab those things for ourselves.

another, it can be seen as a form of bringing on judgment that only God can give. When one lies, it can be seen as an attempt to be above the truth. Cheating on a test could be an attempt to appear "wise."

The Bible's answer to the question *Where does sin come from?* is that it comes from both outside pressures and our own desires. Adam and Eve are tempted by the outside influence of the serpent, but they also cave in to their inward longings. And the effects are devastating. They get cut off from God, their home, even themselves. Feeling shame for the first time, they cover their nakedness. Even the ground is cursed (Gen 3). And as the second story shows, sin affects the family.

Story 2. Pursuing violence. Adam and Eve's son Cain feels jealousy towards his brother Abel. Cain kills Abel, committing the first act of violence. He is cut off from God and from others as he wanders the earth (Gen 4:1-16).

Story 3. Taking the whole world down. Soon the whole human population is full of wickedness (Gen 6–9). So God sends a flood that covers the whole earth. Noah, finding favor with God, escapes the flood via the ark. Only he, his family, and some of every species of animal are saved. In this story, sin not only destroys human relationships, but almost all of creation as well.

The First Manslaughter
— J. Schuetz-Wolff

Story 4. Alienation. The snowball continues. Like Noah's ark, the Tower of Babel involves the whole world (Gen 11:1-9). Here, the people want to make a name for themselves by building a tower that reaches to the heavens. Their efforts are stalled when the Lord confuses their common language so that, speaking in different tongues, they can't understand each other. Community is broken, and the people scatter apart from each other.

In all these stories, we see sin breaking relationships between humans and God, among one another, and between themselves and the created world. That's the problem with sin. And it's so slippery because we don't set out to break relationships. We set out—in sometimes very subtle ways—to be God. It's obvious in the first and the last stories. In the middle two stories, where violence is the problem, this violence is perhaps the most extreme way we try to be God, taking life into our own hands.

Ira Melnichuk/iStockphoto/Thinkstock

Truth and consequences

Rosella: Sin is knowing the good you ought to do and not doing it.

Tara: Sin is to do evil things—disobeying God or hurting people.

Luke: I think sometimes sin becomes this barrier that interferes with our relationship with God—and others too. I used to think that when I sinned God would be displeased with me and just withdraw. But as he said to Adam and Eve, God asks me, "Where are you, Luke?" When I'm hiding in the bushes, God comes after me and pursues me. I love that.

The problem infects everything

Sin has devastating results in our lives. Unfortunately, however, many of us don't want to talk about it. We may want to talk about how horrible Hitler was, but we don't want to talk about how we bad-mouthed the new kid in school or how we stole a CD from someone. These sin stories, on the other hand, paint a clear picture of the relationships sin ruins, and its snowball effect on all of humanity.

Sometimes we are the victim instead of the offender—the sinned against rather than the sinner. Sometimes we're Cain and sometimes we're Abel, and sometimes we're a mixture of both. Sometimes we are tremendously influenced by outside forces, and sometimes it's nobody's fault but our own. But one thing is clear: it's around us and in us in many different ways.

Part of being made in God's image is the gift of free will. Adam and Eve—and all of us—have choices. And God does not force us to do anything. God wants us to make the right choice out of love and gratitude, and in order for that choice to be free, God also had to give us the freedom to choose evil. So a tension remains. How can God guarantee that everything will work out in the end, and at the same time give us the freedom to choose? How can justice win out and God's kingdom come if God refuses to force our obedience and continues to give us the right to mess things up?

Because of the great power of sin and its ability to mess up the system, sometimes the choice to obey God is very difficult. It feels like we really aren't free to choose. Evil affects individuals, creating chaos and heartache for them and their relationships. But it is also true that evil can be a part of whole systems—governments, institutions, organizations, and even something as simple as a group of friends. This may be what the New Testament refers to when it talks about "the powers" or "rulers" (see 1 Cor 2:6; Eph 1:20-21; Col 2:15).

How is sin controlling your life? What relationships is it tearing apart? To whom will you go for help?

If God controls the world, is it more like the control of a well-oiled machine, or the control of a loving parent? And who's to blame when things seem "out of control"?

grace:
the freely given, unmerited favor and love of God

Remember your junior high school or middle school years? There is this group thing that can happen—pecking orders, who's cool, who's not, people compromising their morals just to get into a group. Those are powers. It's not that having a group is always evil or that any one individual in a group sets out specifically to be mean. But what starts out as good or at least neutral can turn ugly. There, too, the power of sin can be especially devastating.

The judgment is the grace. So how does God respond to this awful power of evil? God responds with grace and love (or, God responds like a loving parent). God is not some white-haired, stern figure just waiting with glee to zap us when we sin. There are negative consequences when we sin, that is true, but these consequences also help bring us back into relationship with God. Cain is a good example. Cain was marked and had to wander the earth for his sin. But the mark also meant that no one could kill him. The flood was a terrible consequence of sin. But Noah and his family were saved and the earth was washed clean to start again. Finally, the people building the Tower of Babel were forced to quit their project. But what would have happened if they kept trying? In each of these early "sin" stories, the judgment was also the grace.

A central theme in the Story, which we'll be looking at in the next chapters, is how God works with the problem of sin. Sin brings its problems and its judgment, and it is everywhere. But far greater than the power of sin are God's power and willingness to heal and forgive, and to bring us to where we were created to be. The real story is this . . . God jumping through hoops and bending over backwards to show how deeply God loves us and wants us! We do, however, have to take sin seriously. If we see the problem of sin as only something we commit against God, then we will only emphasize the part of the Story that deals with our relationship with God. Then our main job

It's like going to jail for driving drunk. It's a judgment, but what if it is the only way you can get sober or keep yourself from killing someone? —*Mary*

is deciding whether or not we believe in Jesus. But, if the problem is broken relationships, not only with God but also with others, self, and creation, then salvation (see page 43, 115–120) addresses and heals all of those relationships.

God understood the implications of this awful sin mess. God had a plan. And that plan is the next part of the Story.

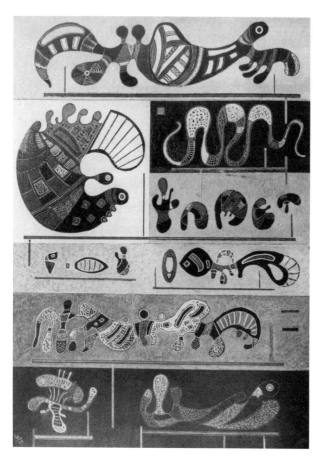

Fruits on the Tree of Knowledge —W. Kandinsky

Summing it up:

- **God is the creator of a good universe.** Though we can't prove it scientifically, we take by faith that God created everything. From the Bible, we understand that the created world is good. In particular, people—both male and female—are created in God's image.

- **God is both beyond knowing and knowable.** The Bible gives us two accounts of creation, not because there were two creations but because it was one way to show how God is both all-powerful and yet personal and close.

- **Sin breaks relationship between us and God, self, others, and all creation.** It's more than just hurting God's feelings. When we sin, relationships are hurt. Sin takes many forms, and it is found everywhere, both in individuals and in whole systems. Sometimes we are the sinners, and at other times we are the ones who are sinned against.

- **Judgment and grace are flip sides of the same coin.** From the beginning of the Bible, we see that God's judgment on sin is not mean-spirited punishment. It is always tied to God's desire to restore right relationships with God, our inner selves, others, and creation.

a **spiritual discipline** to practice:

Write the ABCs along the left-hand side of a piece of paper. Then list one or two names or descriptions of God for each letter. Your list might look like this: A = almighty, awesome, all-powerful; B = beautiful, bountiful; etc.

Topics in chapter 2

- **God chooses people**
- **God's providence**
- **Salvation**
- **Leaving slavery**
- **New way of being**
- **Good rules for living**
- **Holy war—let God defend you**
- **Worship**
- **Shalom**

Story line:
Abraham and Sarah
Moses
God rescues Israelites from slavery
Ten Commandments

2. God Creates Again

Where is God in all of this? If sin is everywhere, what does that mean? And how does God respond? The good news is that God does respond, as he did right there at the beginning of human history. God takes to creating again. Only this time, God creates not a world, but a group of people who know and obey God.

Try to imagine this: You are an ordinary man in the Middle East about 4,000 years ago. You're sitting by a campfire with your wife, and you hear a voice. You don't see anything, but you sense something—outside of you, but inside of you as well. Is it indigestion? Or is it someone, Someone, speaking to you? The voice continues. It wants you to drop everything and just start moving to some new place you don't know about. You check the bushes. Nobody there. You pinch yourself. Nope. Not dreaming. You sense that something extraordinary is going on.

God calls Abraham. That is the story of Abraham. In ways we can only imagine, God communicated with this man and his wife, Sarah, telling them to drop everything and start walking to, well, wherever. But why them? The Bible speaks of God choosing Abraham's family for a special mission (Gen 12). It doesn't mean Abraham and his people were God's favorites to the exclusion of all others. In fact, God

If you were to stop the Story right here, I'm not sure I'd want to join. People mess up paradise, sin is everywhere, and it's—a mess. Where is God in all of this? —*Josh*

tells Abraham and Sarah, "In you all the families of the earth shall be blessed" (Gen 12:3). Abraham and his descendants, too, had a choice: Would they obey this Voice?

Does God have favorites?

Rosella: No.

Luke: I see the whole Bible as a story of inclusion. God chose Abraham in order to choose others. All of us are chosen to choose others.

Tara: There's a tradition that says God calls every single person, and Abraham was just the first one to say yes.

God keeps the Story alive. So God creates a people, beginning with Abraham. At first glance, it seems like God has chosen the wrong couple. Abraham and Sarah have no descendants and are way past the age of childbearing. But God does a God thing, and despite some lack of faith (Sarah even laughed in God's face), Isaac is born to them in their old age (Gen 12–18, 21).

God keeps the Story alive through other miraculous interventions. Some Christians call this divine involvement in our lives *providence*. Isaac and Rebekah and their children and grandchildren all made some bad mistakes—they sinned—and yet God stuck with them. (See Gen 12:10-20; Gen 16:1-15; Gen 18:1-15; Gen 26:6-11; Gen 27:1-40; Gen 29:15-30.) God rescued this family despite natural problems like barrenness and human unfaithfulness and stupidity. They were not always the best examples of godliness—yet God used them.

Perhaps the strangest story of providence revolves around Joseph. Already his father Jacob's favorite son, Joseph bragged to his brothers that some day they would bow to him (Gen 37:1-11). The brothers couldn't take it anymore, and so they threw him in a pit and then sold him as a slave to Egypt. But what seemed really bad actually turned out to be what saved this same family.

providence:
a manifestation of divine care or direction

Joseph rose to power as one of Egypt's top leaders. He stored up enough food for a famine that would sweep the entire Middle East. His brothers—the same ones who sold him into slavery—came down to Egypt from Canaan looking for food. They bowed in reverence before Joseph, not knowing this was their own brother. The hated one became the hero. More importantly, through God's providence, the family was kept alive to keep developing God's Story.

Living it out

I was bewildered. The questions kept coming. Five pastors in four weeks posed essentially the same wonderment: Have you considered pastoral ministry? Others ventured similar queries. Several years previous, God had convinced me to make a complete course reversal and follow Jesus, instead of personal narcissism. God, now a divine huckster, appeared to be dealing off the bottom of the deck.

How could I ask my family—two young sons, a daughter, and Idella (who finally had the Christian husband she had prayed for)—to make the tenuous sacrifice of following Jesus into education and ministry? I could not place the initial phone call to Hesston College to inquire about the pastoral ministry program there.

One day, as I returned from work, Idella met me at the door with this comment: "I called Hesston College today." In hindsight, I realize that God succinctly answered a terse personal prayer: let me use my gifts; let me make a difference in people's lives. Pastoral work remains deeply gratifying. The call that evolved 25 years ago, initially resisted, still remains. —*Ruben Chupp, Nappanee, Indiana*

Josh: If you think the only real reason bad things happen to us is for God to use them somehow, it can really mess you up.

Mary: I don't think God makes bad things happen. Our freedom of choice allows it.

Rosella: But God is powerful enough to stop things from happening to people.

Mary: And powerful enough to understand we'll learn from our mistakes.

Tara: God doesn't cause bad things—sin does. But God can turn even bad situations into something good.

Mike: Sometimes God has to discipline us by letting our consequences really happen to us.

Rose: And God does this out of love.

Josh: Then why doesn't God do it all the time—turn a bad situation into something good?

Tara: Maybe we just don't see it. Joseph probably couldn't see God at work when he was sitting in the dungeon. No way.

salvation:

God's work to bring creation back to what it was meant to be.

Included in salvation are at least three strands of "good news": God heals broken relationships, freeing us from the power and consequences of sin; God makes us into new people; and God works in us to bring God's healing and hope to our world.

Salvation is really at the heart of the Story and comes up over and over in this book. See pages 43, 66, 75–77, and 115–120 for more.

Salvation, part 1: leaving slavery

It would seem like everything is just fine. Jacob (Israel) and his children and grandchildren moved from Canaan to Egypt to escape the widespread famine (Gen 46). For a while, the Story seems on track. The family grows and prospers. But a new pharaoh comes to power who doesn't know about Joseph and his family (Exod 1:8-14). He takes one look at these foreigners who are doing so well and he enslaves them. The slavery was torture, and the oppression severe. But the more the Israelites were oppressed, the more they multiplied. So Pharaoh decrees that every Israelite baby boy should be thrown into the Nile River (Exod 1:22). Now the Story is in trouble like it has never been before. Now it is time for God to show not just providence, but salvation.

The God who had been merciful all along, the God who had showered the Israelites with steadfast love, is the same God who hears their cries for help. The help comes in the most unlikely form: an Israelite baby floating in a basket in the Nile River. His name is Moses. His mother had hidden him there to escape the fate of the other slave babies. God honors her step of faith. Pharaoh's daughter picks Moses up out of the water, and the baby slated for death becomes the new son of the palace.

Even though Moses grew up in Pharaoh's palace, he somehow identifies with his own people. One day he sees an Egyptian beating one of his kinsfolk and it is more than he can bear. He kills the Egyptian taskmaster and then flees for his own life into the wilderness (Exod 2).

The Voice. Pharaoh didn't find him, but God does. It is there in the desert that Moses sees a bush that is on fire, yet not consumed (Exod 3). From the bush comes a voice—the Voice who has spoken

Moses murders a guy. That always intrigues me. And God didn't just shut him off. Years later Moses holds the Law in his hands that says, "Do not kill." Amazing. —*Luke*

From what kinds of oppression do you need deliverance? Looking back over your life, where has God rescued you?

to his ancestors. "I have observed the misery of my people who are in Egypt," God says. "I know their sufferings, and I have come down to deliver them from the Egyptians. . . . So come, I will send you to Pharaoh to bring my people, the Israelites, out of Egypt" (Exod 3:7-10). God is going to rescue the Israelites from their slavery with one of the members of Pharaoh's own household!

Moses, reluctantly at first, agrees to his assignment and goes back to Egypt. Along with his brother Aaron, he asks Pharaoh to let the slaves go free. When Pharaoh refuses, the Lord sends 10 plagues on Egypt—plagues that miraculously do not hurt the slaves (Exod 5:1–12:32). The last plague is the deadliest. The angel of death comes to every household, and in every household the firstborn dies. The only ones spared from this terrible fate are the families who put the blood of a lamb on their doorpost.

I never liked this story. Why should someone die for their family's mistakes? —*Mary*

God's name, Yahweh

At the burning bush, God reveals God's personal name, Yahweh, to Moses. Roughly translated, Yahweh means "I AM who I AM" or "I will be who I will be" (Exod 3:13-14), and is translated as Lord in most English Bibles. This name is so special that even today many Jews do not pronounce the name, and many write it without its vowels—YHWH.

In the ancient world, to reveal one's name to another was to initiate a relationship and become vulnerable to that person. That the Creator of the universe would take the initiative to proclaim this personal name to Moses was an unheard-of step toward building relationship between God and humans.

Later Jesus identifies himself as the "I AM." In the book of John, Jesus says, "I am the living bread" (6:51), "I am the true vine" (15:1), "I am the good shepherd" (10:11), and "I am the resurrection and the life" (11:25). His choice of words was no accident; most Jews avoided the phrase "I AM" out of respect for God. Jesus was calling himself by the same sacred name reserved only for Yahweh.

Pharaoh finally decides to let the slaves go free (Exod 12:33-37). Here the Bible includes an important detail: Other people, probably non-Israelite slaves, join God's people in the exodus (v. 38). As God has told Abraham, God cares not only for the children of Abraham, but for all who suffered under the oppression.

Pharaoh, however, changes his mind. It is too convenient to have thousands of hardworking slaves at his fingertips. He sends an army after the helpless, unarmed slaves to bring them back. As they hear the chariots charging after them, the slaves size up their situation. With Pharaoh's army behind them and the Red Sea in front of them, they know they are trapped. But Moses says, "Do not be afraid, stand firm, and see the deliverance that the LORD will accomplish for you today. The LORD will fight for you, and you have only to keep still" (Exod 14:13b-14; see page 36 for a discussion of holy war).

See the Confession of Faith summary of Article 10 about making disciples out of all nations on page 175.

Miriam Dances —Ray Dirks

God does it all. As difficult as it is, they have no choice. Moses raises up his staff. The pillar of cloud that guided them moves behind them, and a strong east wind blows. Miraculously the waters part. Amazed, the people cross through on dry ground. When the Egyptian army follows them into the sea, the waters go back together and the Egyptian army is drowned. Safe on the other shore, Moses's sister Miriam leads them in a celebration to God (Exod 15:20).

It was here, on the other side of the Red Sea, that this motley crew of mixed peoples became a people. It was here, having experienced such a dramatic rescue, that they bonded as one—the Israelites. They had experienced the salvation of God. This deliverance from slavery would be the Story that would sustain the people of Israel throughout their history. It was at the center of who they were.

How hard is it for you to stand still and let God fight for you like the slaves did? Should this way of living apply only to our individual lives or should we also trust God when we have national enemies? Check out the Confession of Faith summary for Article 22 on page 177 and discuss what it means.

The exodus story is retold and celebrated often in the Old Testament. At least six of the Psalms (78, 105, 106, 114, 135, 136) remember God's deliverance of the people from Egypt. The prophets often refer to the exodus when they call the people back to God (Isa 11:16; Jer 2:6; 7:22-25; Ezek 20:6, 10). Passover was the Jews' annual commemoration of the exodus. It was at the Passover meal that Jesus explains the "new covenant" through his own body and blood (Luke 22:20; see also page 47, 128–129).

Holy war

Everyone in the ancient world believed in something called "holy war," where the gods helped people fight their wars. The Israelites believed in holy war, too, but with one major difference. Everyone else believed that you had to fight as a way of helping the gods. But the Israelites looked back to the Red Sea as the true way of fighting. With the Egyptians hot on their trail, Moses told the people to "stand still and the Lord will fight for you" (Exod 14:13-14). So all through the early days, God's people did holy war that way. They understood that the Lord did not need them to fight.

While in the Red Sea event the Israelites were different from all other peoples in that they didn't fight, they were like other ancient peoples in that they did understand that other humans were to be killed. And many Christians today still struggle with that part of holy war—the ban. In holy war, everything about the enemy was to be destroyed—every cow, every horse, and, yes, every person. Part of obedience to God was killing everything. This was done in holy war for two reasons. First, the Israelites were not tempted to go to war to gain wealth, because all the wealth was to be destroyed. Second, it got rid of all idol worship because there were no foreign people there to tempt them to worship other gods. And in original holy war, the Lord drowned the Egyptian army.

Other Christians struggle with holy war because they can't decide which kind of holy war to follow. Do we follow the original holy war where God does all the fighting, like at the Red Sea? This would mean that Christians would not fight in an army for their country but, instead, trust God to take care of them. Or do we follow the holy wars that happened later in the Old Testament, where the Israelites fought and killed other people?

The Israelites slipped from the original way of doing holy war very quickly. They moved from fighting with God (Judg 4) to fighting for God (2 Sam 24), and when they did, they had fewer and fewer successes. They became so unfaithful to God's intent that in 587 BCE God actually fought with the Babylonians against them, culminating in the people's exile to Babylon (Jer 21:1-6).

Why is this important? Because Jesus chose to use holy war in the original way. Jesus demonstrated on the cross the most effective way to defeat evil. He submitted himself in obedience to God and let God take care of him. In the short view of things, Jesus' enemies won. They killed him. But in the longer view, Jesus defeated, once and for all, the evil that enslaves us. And God gave him victory through the resurrection.

> *In the short view of things, Jesus' enemies won. They killed him. But in the longer view, Jesus defeated, once and for all, the evil that enslaves us.*

The apostle Paul understood this original way of fighting evil. He writes in Romans 12:19-21, "Beloved, never avenge yourselves, but leave room for the wrath of God; for it is written, 'Vengeance is mine, I will repay, says the Lord.' No, 'if your enemies are hungry, feed them; if they are thirsty, give them something to drink; for by doing this you will heap burning coals on their heads.' Do not be overcome by evil, but overcome evil with good."

Today there are people who say they fight because God tells them to. Even many Christians try to justify war by referring to the wars in the Old Testament. They believe that being a part of God's people and being a part of their country or political party is the same thing. Holy war according to the Bible is not like this at all. God's first intention is for us simply to trust God. Judgment or vengeance belongs to the Lord (Rom 12:19-20). The exodus story is a clear example of this.

Salvation: spiritual or physical? Sometimes we like to think of salvation as just an individual, spiritual thing. In the exodus story, salvation means physical freedom from an oppression that is literally killing the people. God does care about the spiritual oppression that we all suffer because of sin. But God also cares about physical injustice and oppression. If salvation brings back together everything that sin breaks apart, then somehow it must mean good news for those who suffer physically as well as those who suffer spiritually.

Salvation, part 2: a new way of being

Physical deliverance wasn't the end of the story for the Israelites. They were in great need of deliverance from the sin and messed-up thinking inside them. Ironically, the former slaves begin complaining about the lack of food almost as soon as they are out of Egypt. They long to go back to the "fleshpots" of Egypt (Exod 16:3). This was a case of mass amnesia, as they remembered only the security and not the hardship of the good old days. They not only needed physical deliverance from death-dealing slavery, but they also needed new hearts, and they needed to know how to be the people of God.

In the wilderness, the Lord not only provides food for them (see Exod 16), but also sets out to help them understand a whole new way of living. God begins with the Ten Commandments. At Mount Sinai, the same place where Moses met the burning bush, the Lord speaks to Moses and gives him these words for living together in peaceful community (Exod 19–20). The commandments were—and are—a way to respond to the incredible act of God's grace in saving the slaves from their slavery. In introducing the commandments, God reminds the people: "I am the LORD your God, who brought you out of the land of Egypt, out of the house of slavery . . ." (Exod 20:1).

The Israelites were called to rely completely on God in the desert, accepting God's salvation and letting God fight their battles. Does God still desire such radical trust on your part? How does it show in your life?

Shalom, a different way to live. The Ten Commandments are also words that, when followed, bring about a community of trust and safety. This is far different from the society the Israelites were used to back in Egypt, and it is a far cry from many of the communities we live in today. The commandments are words of *shalom*—the Hebrew word that some translate as "peace." It means much more, however, than inward peace with God, or not going to war. To have shalom means to be in right relationship with neighbors. It means everyone has a chance to work and make a decent living, everyone has enough to eat and a house to sleep in. Shalom happens when we are at peace with God, with our inner selves, with one another, and with creation. In that sense, it depicts the world before sin has a chance to break apart all those precious relationships.

Tablets Given to Moses —Raphael

Luke: Sometimes people see the Bible as nothing but a bunch of rules.

Josh: Yeah, and God is some mean judge up in the sky who loves to zap us.

Mary: But is that really being fair to God? Can't the rules have some good purpose?

Michele: Mary has a point. Take the rules about manna, the food God gave the people in the wilderness. The people were told to gather only enough manna for one day's supply. The day before Sabbath, the people were to gather enough for two days, so that they could truly rest on the Sabbath. That was the rule. If they gathered more than they needed, their precious food supply got wormy and unfit to eat. A picky rule from a picky God? No, they had this rule so they could learn to trust God every day for their food. The rule also taught them the importance of Sabbath rest (Exod 16).

The Ten Commandments

Then God spoke all these words:

2   am the LORD your God, who brought you out of the land of Egypt, out of the house of slavery; ³ you shall have no other gods before me.

4   You shall not make for yourself an idol, whether in the form of anything that is in heaven above, or that is on the earth beneath, or that is in the water under the earth. . . .

7   You shall not make wrongful use of the name of the LORD your God, for the LORD will not acquit anyone who misuses his name.

8   Remember the sabbath day, and keep it holy. . . . ¹¹ For in six days the LORD made heaven and earth, the sea, and all that is in them, but rested the seventh day; therefore the LORD blessed the sabbath day and consecrated it.

12 Honor your father and your mother, so that your days may be long in the land that the LORD your God is giving you.

13 You shall not murder.

14 You shall not commit adultery.

15 You shall not steal.

16 You shall not bear false witness against your neighbor.

17 You shall not covet your neighbor's house; you shall not covet your neighbor's wife, or male or female slave, or ox, or donkey, or anything that belongs to your neighbor.

—Exodus 20:1-17

A different way to worship. By accepting the Ten Commandments the people, in essence, declare God as their ruler. The Israelites, in contrast to all the surrounding cultures, are led and governed by an invisible force. Yes, there was a visible pillar of cloud by day and a pillar of fire by night, but even in this visual display there was a mystery. God was seen and yet hidden. Here in the wilderness the Lord is calling the shots and the people follow. When the pillar starts to move, the people start to move—no questions asked (Num 10:11-12).

Even the worship space—the tabernacle—is nothing more than an elaborate tent, ready to follow the invisible, almighty Presence (Exod 26). This stands in stark contrast to the idol worship and temple system that will later tempt God's people (Jer 7), where they think God can be housed in a permanent fixture and manipulated like an ordinary piece of wood (Isa 44:9-20). But out here in the wilderness, God is free, and God is in control.

Tabernacle in the Wilderness
—G. Castellino

The motive for worship is also different. Before, the people prayed to Egyptian gods so they could prosper. If you prayed just right, the gods were obliged to give you fertile fields and lots of children. But in the wilderness, the Israelites worship God because God acted first, in history, to save them. Before they deserved it, God rescued them from slavery. Before they deserved it, God provided for their every need. So instead of fearing the gods or working to manipulate the gods, the wilderness people love God. The *Shema*, the heart of the entire Law that Jesus also quotes to his disciples, states:

> Hear, O Israel: The LORD is our God, the LORD alone. You shall love the LORD your God with all your heart, and with all your soul, and with all your might (Deut 6:4-5; Mark 12:29-30).

Why do you worship? What if you know you are supposed to feel thankful and worship God for that reason, but you just don't feel it?

A different kind of economics. The love and worship of God is also connected to right living (Mic 6:6-8). God wants to form a new society where everyone has a chance to experience shalom. To reflect the rest God took after creation and the rest God gave to the slaves in Egypt, the Lord makes a Sabbath for all creation. Not only is every seventh day to be a day of rest. Every seven years the ground is to rest from crops and tilling. Every seven years all debts are to be forgiven and slaves are to be set free. These rules give "rest" to those who have fallen on hard times. And every 50 years, the Jubilee year (Lev 25:10), all the land is to go back to its original owners. Such a system will "level the playing field," while also leaving people free to be productive and industrious.

Taken together, the exodus and wilderness events give us a clear picture of salvation. God rescued people from both physical and spiritual oppression. As Christians, we may look back and say that this salvation was woefully lacking, because *real* salvation has come only with Jesus. But Jesus' understanding of salvation was not that much different. He too was concerned about physical and spiritual healing. And, like the exodus-Sinai events, Jesus brought a salvation that is both for the individual and for the people. He gathered 12 disciples around him (Mark 3:13-19); these would be the start of the church, the new people of God.

What does salvation mean?

There are many Hebrew (Old Testament) and Greek (New Testament) words that we translate into English as salvation. *Save* in the Old Testament can mean deliver, bring to safety, redeem, vindicate, help in time of distress, rescue, or set free. Sometimes it's very specific and individual. Hannah, for example, couldn't have children and was "saved" when God gave her Samuel. Sometimes salvation is more general, as in Psalm 33:19, where the people pray that the Lord will save Israel from famine and death.

Salvation in the Old Testament can mean physical or spiritual deliverance (see Ezek 36:22-32; 37:1-14; Jer 31:31-34), but it is always clear that it comes from God, not from some natural event or human force (Ps 33:16-17).

The most commonly used word in the New Testament for salvation means to save and to heal. Jesus used the same word to say, "Your faith has made you well" (Luke 17:19; Mark 10:52), that he used to say, "Your faith has saved you" (Luke 7:50). As in the Old Testament, there is more than one layer of meaning. When Peter walks on the water, he cries to Jesus to save him (Matt 14:22-33). On one level, Peter needs to be saved from drowning, but it's also obvious from the story that Peter needs to be rescued from his doubt and fear.

Throughout the Bible, salvation is experienced as people trust God (Ps 22:4). We are "saved by faith" through God's initiative, not our own efforts, even though salvation motivates us to respond in "good works" (Eph. 2:8-10). God's saving work in our lives motivates us to love, caring for the poor and oppressed (Lev. 19:33; Deut. 10:18-19).

Salvation leads to changed behavior. Jesus tells the woman caught in adultery, "Neither do I condemn you. Go your way, and from now on do not sin again" (John 8:11). Touched by Jesus' visit to his house, Zacchaeus volunteers to give back the money he took from people. "Today salvation has come to this house," Jesus replies (Luke 19:9).

Summing it up

- **God begins to solve humanity's sin problem by creating a people.** God called Abraham and Sarah, whose obedience continues the Story of God's working in the world.

- **God calls everyone in one way or another.** We have all been chosen for a mission, just like Abraham and Sarah were. That doesn't mean we're God's favorites. It means we have been given a task of bringing God's blessing to the world.

- **God initiates a relationship with us.** God initiated a covenant with Abraham and Sarah and their descendants. God renewed the relationship when God heard the people's cries in Egypt, rescued them from slavery, and formed them into a people. God continued to relate to humanity through Jesus and continues to work through the church and in our lives today.

- **Our worship is a response of love to God.** Worship is not a series of rituals to persuade God to give us favors. This is because God has taken the initiative to act in history.

- **God's people are called to radical trust in God.** In their escape from Egypt the people of Israel learned they can depend solely on God for protection, rather than fighting their enemies themselves.

- **The people of God are a community founded on shalom.** The Ten Commandments and the other Old Testament laws point to a society where all have hope, dignity, and a chance to care for themselves economically. Jesus continued this emphasis in his own life and teachings.

What will the Israelites do with their newfound freedom, now that they've been liberated? Will it be a quick and easy trip to the Promised Land? And what will God do when things go bad? Read on . . .

- **Salvation is both physical and spiritual, and both individual and corporate.** The exodus and wilderness events show that God wants to deliver all of our lives from the destructiveness of sin. Jesus also demonstrated this. If sin breaks relationships between God, self, others, and creation, then our salvation brings renewed, healed relationships not only with God, but also with ourselves, others, and creation.

Moses and the Burning Bush
—F. Hoffman

a **spiritual discipline** to practice:

Go to Deuteronomy 26:5-10. Rewrite this little story as your own story. You can write about your ancestors ("a wandering Aramean was my ancestor"), a few sentences about your oppression, and then how God rescued you in the past or is rescuing you right now. Finally, you can write about your new "land flowing with milk and honey" and about what you are going to do in response to God's rescue ("now I bring the first of the fruit of the ground"). If you don't think you have begun to feel God's rescue, you can write about that instead.

Covenant

God did what it took to create a people who would learn how to love and trust God and live in a peaceful, just community with each other. One of the specific ways God helped them understand such relationships was through covenants. In much the same way that ancient rulers made political alliances with each other or with their subjects, God made covenants with people. Some were unconditional, where God promised blessings no matter what. Others were conditional, where God would bless the people if they were faithful.

Here are some of the main covenants in the Bible:

- Noah (Gen 8:21-22; 9:8-17)

- Abraham (Gen 12:1-3; 15:4-20; 17:2-8)

- Sinai covenant through Moses (Exod 19:3-6; 20:1-17)

- Shechem covenant through Joshua (Josh 24)

- David (2 Sam 7:11b-16)

- Jeremiah's vision of a new covenant (Jer 31:31-34)

- Ezekiel's vision of a new covenant (Ezek 36)

- Ezra's covenant renewal (Neh 10:28-31)

- Jesus' new covenant (Matt 26:28; Mark 14:24; Luke 22:20)

These covenants established a relationship between God and people. While each party had to hold up its end of the bargain, only God initiated the covenant. Often, God stayed with the covenant agreement even when the people failed to do their part (Isa 54:10). Sometimes God was so hurt by what the people did that God considered starting all over again (e.g., Exod 32). But each time, the people or their leaders would plead with God until God decided to stick with the people after all. In the Old Testament, this is called God's "steadfast love." The New Testament often calls it "grace" (see page 24).

Topics in chapter 3

- **Faith as a long journey**
- **The temptation to be like the others**
- **How we read the Bible**
- **God as the only true ruler**
- **Judgment is also grace—new starts**
- **Keeping pure in a dirty world**

Story line:

Israelites in the wilderness
Entering the Promised Land
Judges and kings
Israel in exile
Rebuilding Jerusalem

3. Competing Gods

It would seem, at first glance, that everything is perfect. The Israelites have been saved from slavery in Egypt and are being saved from slavery thinking in the wilderness. What was once a crowd has become a people, birthed at the Red Sea. It is all so simple now. The people can trust God for all their needs, worship God out of love and gratitude, and live in a shalom justice community.

If only they could. The Israelites made many mistakes along the way. The old ways of being, thinking, and living were hard to give up. The new way of obeying an invisible Presence who didn't function like the Egyptian gods was frustrating, scary, and sometimes downright mystifying. And the people mess up—miserably.

God takes the long road

As in our own lives, faith was a journey for the Israelites. The Israelites did manage to get to the border of the Promised Land—but sadly, they couldn't go in (see Num 13–14 for the story). They could have gone in, had they had faith enough to trust that God would take care of them. Twelve spies go into the land and see that it is incredibly fertile, "flowing with milk and honey." But, said 10 of them, the people

Okay, we're at the Promised Land. Can we go home now? —*Tara*

Tara: Why are we emphasizing God making a people?

Mike: Right. Why didn't God just zap sin and be done with it?

Mary: Couldn't Jesus have just come earlier than he did?

Michele: God does seem to take the long road. Why?

Josh: I hate these questions.

Tara: Isn't the exodus and the wilderness like our own experience? I always thought that as soon as I got baptized, I'd go straight to the Promised Land. Everything would be great.

Michele: I thought I would never be tempted again. Did you think that?

Luke: Oh yeah.

Mike: I've heard people say that Satan tempts you more after you are baptized.

Michele: No one told me that, and it really threw me. I doubted my baptism for awhile.

Rosella: I'm an old woman and I'm still in the wilderness sometimes.

Luke: Maybe there's more to Christianity than just "getting in."

there are giants and the cities fortified. Who were they to go against those kinds of odds?

The 10 advise the people that their entry will be suicidal. The other two spies, Joshua and Caleb, say that with the Lord's help they can enter. Was this not the same God who performed holy war for them at the Red Sea (see page 36), who gave them manna every day, who led them by the mysterious pillar of cloud and fire? How many miraculous events do they need?

Judgment is the grace. In the end, the 10 doubters win out, and God tells the people that for their lack of faith they will now have to wander the desert for 40 more years. But like before, God's judgment is also the grace. The people need a stretch of time to figure out who their God, Yahweh, is. They need this time to learn to really trust. During these 40 years, the Lord will continue to re-form this infant people. God knows Canaan will be filled with plenty of its own new challenges.

Mike: So the Israelites are just like us—following God, but screwing up all the same.

Tara: It seems so easy to say, "I trust God," but it's a lot more difficult to put into practice.

Luke: But like the Israelites, we do get better. We have the Holy Spirit to help us move on and grow up. I don't believe that we have to be stuck forever in a cycle of unfaithfulness.

Mary: But it's easier said than done.

Finally, a new home. After 40 years and the death of Moses, the Israelites enter Canaan, the Promised Land, under the leadership of Joshua (Josh 3–4). Through God's holy war they conquer many areas, but not all of them. So instead of settling on land that has no other occupants, they settle among pagan peoples who have different understandings about the divine world (Josh 17:16-18; Judg 2:1-3; 3:4).

The inhabitants of Canaan rely upon gods called the Baals to grant them survival through good harvests and many children. The Israelites are used to herding sheep in the solitary wilderness. New neighbors and new agricultural demands put pressure on them to adopt Baal worship. The pressure is just too much. Combining Yahweh worship with Baal worship, they worship idols so that their crops will grow (Judg 10:6ff.). God's ethics of living a shalom community (see page 39) were often forgotten. The people even began to give their children Baal names, just to be on the safe side (Judg 8:33-35). And this gradual mixing of two religions, called syncretism, became their undoing (Jer 7:16–8:3).

syncretism:

gradually mixing two religions together, so that you are practicing both —*Michele*

Luke: Many Christians combine their Christianity with love of country. So loving God gets mixed up with nationalism.

Tara: It's all very subtle. We live in a culture of violence. Now is that a pagan religion?

Luke: We are also taken up with consumerism. Buying things is the cool thing to do. Combine that with Christianity and you get prosperity gospel: If I'm really faithful, God will make me a millionaire.

Josh: Sign me up.

Tara: But we can't be totally separate from our culture either.

Michele: At what point is the mixing of our culture and faith wrong?

Mike: When you start to put the cultural boundaries around God.

Luke: When you begin to domesticate God. Isn't that what idol worship is? When you make God liberal, conservative, or white, or pizza-eating.

Tara: Or when you won't do anything radical for God anymore.

Steadfast love. Israel's merciful and holy God refuses to give up on the people. This time God provides "judges"—leaders who administer government under God. As the book of Judges tells it, there is a predictable cycle under these leaders:

1. The Israelites fail to live up to the promises they made to God.

2. This sin brings about oppression, as God allows other groups to capture them and rule them with an iron hand.

3. In desperation, the Israelites cry out to the Lord.

4. Moved by their pleas, God acts by appointing a judge to lead them.

5. The judge helps deliver them through a modified holy war (see page 36). Even more important, the judge reminds them of the exodus and God's gracious leading and providence.

6. But as soon as the judge dies, the people forget. They forget God and they forget the Story. They slip back into their old ways (see Judg 3–4 for examples).

We want a king. The up and down cycle of the judges gets old. So the Israelites ask one of their judges, Samuel, to anoint a human ruler for them. Enemies were threatening invasion, and Samuel's own sons were rotten judges. Besides, all the peoples around them had kings. Samuel, however, remembers the wilderness dream that God would be their king. He asks God what he should do. "They are not rejecting you," says the Lord, "but they are rejecting me."

Samuel Annoints Saul —J. Pander

Samuel warns the people that human kings will abuse their power, tax the people, take their best fields and crops, and eventually take their sons and daughters as slaves. But his words fall on deaf ears; the Israelites still demand a human king. Samuel goes back to the Lord, who now instructs him to do what the people want. (See 1 Sam 8 for the whole story.)

This sets up an interesting problem for us today. What was God's will for the people? Did it matter to God whether or not they got a human king? Or did God really want them to have a king? And why didn't God simply force them into obedience or perform some incredible miracle to prove that they were safe and secure with Yahweh, the Lord, as their only king?

These questions are all the more complicated and important because the book of 1 Samuel records two different reactions to monarchy. In the anti-monarchy strand (1 Sam 8; 10:17-27; 12), God pronounces judgment on the people for choosing a king. Saul, the first king to be anointed, is shown to be a bumbling fool. In the pro-monarchy strand (1 Sam 9:1–10:16; 10:27b–11:15), Saul is filled with divine spirit so that he prophesies and leads the Israelites in successful holy war. He even spares the lives of those who spoke against him. So which strand is right? (See sidebar: "When the Bible story comes in different versions." See also "Tips on using the Bible" on page 163.)

When have you been aware that God gives you free choice?

How God reigns. In Samuel's day, God wanted to be the only ruler. God could have forced the people to fall into line under divine kingship. Instead, in love and mercy, God gave them free choice. And they chose to have a human king. God eventually worked out divine purposes through the royal line of David. This kind of thing happens in story after story in the Bible. God has a Plan A, the people choose another way, and God moves to Plan B.

How do we know that God's direct rule was God's best plan and that the monarchy was God's second choice? We don't know for sure, but we can look at what happened in the Story. The monarchy helped shape the Israelites' false idea that God belonged only to their nation.

Luke: Another paradox, right? God is all-powerful and yet gives people the free choice.

Tara: And God chooses to stay with the people.

Michele: Even when the monarchy went sour and came tumbling down on the Israelites.

Luke: God always has another plan. The kings went bad, so God brings in the prophets. It finally gets to the point where God says, "Okay, I'm going to give my own son." It's like God always has a plan. I love that.

When the Bible story comes in different versions

Many people find it upsetting that the Bible sometimes carries two strands of the same story. What does this mean? Is one strand right and the other wrong? Does this mean the Bible is not God's inspired Word?

It helps to understand how stories worked in the ancient world. Back then, historical accuracy was viewed differently than it is today. It was important to communicate the essence of a story, using the facts to lift out the symbolism and special meaning of the bigger story. The New Testament writer John, for example, put the story of Jesus chasing the moneychangers from the temple at the beginning of Jesus' ministry; the gospels of Matthew, Mark, and Luke put it near the end. John was not as concerned about when the event actually happened as he was about the meaning of the temple. Since one of his main themes in the book is that Jesus, not the temple, is the center of faith, he chose to tell the story at the beginning.

Most of the stories in the Old Testament were passed on by word of mouth for hundreds of years before they were written on animal skins or papyrus. Story was so important to the people's identity that when slightly different versions of the same story would emerge—which was likely when so many different groups recited the same story—the Hebrews kept both stories. Instead of declaring one right and one wrong, the stories were so sacred that the editors would often place them side by side when they were put into writing. They trusted that there was something special in each story; they didn't trust themselves to judge which story was more "true."

They trusted that there was something special in each story; they didn't trust themselves to judge which story was more "true."

Seen in this way, we can still trust the Bible as inspired by God. The stories sit in creative tension with each other, speaking to each other as well as to us. We need to love the Bible enough to study it, talk about the different strands, and use the whole message of the Bible, particularly the life and teachings of Jesus, to help us determine God's will.

Read the Confession of Faith summary of Article 4 about Scripture on page 173.

Can you think of a time in your life when you realized you didn't choose God's original plan for you and so God began working out Plan B in your life?

Are you more comfortable with the God of the wilderness or the God that the monarchy represented? What happens when you only emphasize one or the other?

See the Confession of Faith summary of Article 23 about church and government on page 177.

It nurtured the idea that God can only be found and worshiped in a certain place: their temple. The change happened slowly, and there were a few shining examples of godly kings. But little by little, the God who used to set the agenda in the wilderness became the God who was used to bless the government of the day. The God who used to be worshiped anywhere became the God who could only be found in the temple.

When God was king in the wilderness, the "Jubilee" system made sure everyone had enough and that no one was allowed to hoard or be greedy (see page 42). But under the monarchy, the economic system meant abundance and wealth for some and poverty for others. King Solomon heavily taxed his own people as he built the temple and expanded his own wealth.

Leadership was different, too. In the wilderness, Moses worked with the people to create a free community of shalom. The Israelite kings, by contrast, acted a lot like the pagan kings in the surrounding countries. They oppressed their own people and used religion to justify it (Jer 34:8-22). Having the temple, the kings assumed God was on their side (Jer 7:1-15). The people put more and more faith in their military power than in God doing the fighting for them.

In the end, Samuel's warnings all came true. Shalom was rare under the Israelite kings. It's no surprise, then, that when Jesus came he identified himself with the prophets more than his ancestors, the kings. It was Elijah and Moses who met him on the Mount of Transfiguration, not David and Solomon (Luke 9:28-36). That suggests again that while God sometimes works through human government, our fundamental allegiance must be to God alone.

The prophets kept the vision alive

Even though things have gone wrong in so many ways, God keeps planning for the people's good. Now, instead of judges, God calls up prophets. These men and women speak God's word, especially to the ones in power. They "comfort the afflicted and afflict the comfortable." They confront the kings when they forget about shalom justice for all (Amos 2:6-16; 4). They rail against idol worship (1 Kings 18). They champion the cause of the poor (Jer 5:26-29; Amos 8:4-8).

Who are the prophets God has sent to you? Do you listen?

Over and over again, the prophets remind the people of the Story—especially the exodus—and hold up the vision of shalom (e.g., Amos 3:1-2) and who God is. As a result, they are often persecuted for that vision (Jer 37–38). In many ways, they reflected the kind of ministry Jesus had. Although Jesus was "king," he was a servant whose life and teachings were more in line with the prophets' vision of God than the kings' vision (see pages 67–73).

The kingdom divides. Despite the prophets preaching God's word to the people, the troubles continue for the people of God. Israel's united monarchy lasted only 100 years and three kings. By King Solomon's time, only 400 years after being freed from slavery in

---

How we see Jesus, how we see ourselves

How we view the Story in the Old Testament affects how we view Jesus and how we believe and act as Christians. If the monarchy was what God really desired, then our picture of Jesus would tend to emphasize Jesus as a militant king, and it would be easy to justify a faith that mixes God, wealth, and country. But if the wilderness experience represents the ideal, then we can more easily see Jesus as a servant king who comes to restore a shalom community where everyone can follow God and no country is God's favorite. God's people solve problems nonviolently, trusting in God, not in money or military power. God's people volunteer to live by Jubilee standards so that all may have shalom.

The Prophet Joel Speaks on the Last Judgment —M. Chagall

Living it out

Hope Fellowship is a Christian community and church best understood as a family of neighbors who worship together and share their lives throughout the week across borders of language and culture. We are an Anabaptist community associated with Shalom Mission Communities.

After exploring the theme of God's economy for a year, a group from our community started the Mustard Seed Fund to try and live out what we were learning. Basically, the fund is a group savings account that we use to make zero-interest loans to each other. People can put some of their savings into this fund for a specified period of time to be used to help others in the community. Purposes for loans include reducing high-interest debt, education expenses, travel expenses, or large purchases that would not be possible without the loan. In the future we hope to use this fund, as it grows, to start small businesses that employ and support our community. We see this as a way for us to share with all, as they have need (Acts 2:45). —*Lucas Land, Waco, Texas*

Baal

Other peoples who surrounded the Israelites worshiped gods that the Bible calls Baals. Baal worshipers saw these gods as beings who lived above the sky, who could be influenced by just the right prayers and rituals. In one sense, these Baals had to do their part when the humans did theirs. Yahweh, the Lord, was very different.

God stepped into history, taking the initiative to rescue the slaves from Pharaoh. God was not manipulated into saving them. God loved them. Likewise, the Israelites were to worship God, not to get special favors, but out of thankfulness for God's acts of love.

Egypt, the people are in a slavery of their own making. And now the kingdom divides in two. The 10 northern tribes, Israel, revolt against the two southern tribes, Judah and Benjamin, where the king and Jerusalem are housed.

The division does not bring either nation any closer to God. Both struggle with Baal worship and social injustice (1 Kings 16:29-34; 21:1-9). Both become firm in the belief that God is only their God and can only be found in their territory. Even the reforms led by Kings Hezekiah and Josiah of Judah (2 Kings 18 and 22) are not enough to stave off the judgment of God. Israel falls to Assyria in 722 BCE and the 10 northern tribes are dispersed and lost from history. Judah falls to the Babylonians in 587 BCE.

In the judgment is grace

The people of Judah are taken into exile in Babylon and remain there for 70 years. This is especially painful, but it is very important to their survival as a people. While living in Babylon, they realize that God doesn't have to be worshiped only at the temple. They begin to meet in smaller groups called synagogues, and many actually participate more fully in worship than they did back in Jerusalem. Without the temple

When in your life has judgment gone together with grace?

the people rediscover the Torah, or Law, our first five books of the Bible, and other sacred writings. In order to preserve their identity, they collect, organize, and write down more of their story. In all these ways the people of God, now for the first time called Jews, are being strengthened. They rediscover their identity, as they rediscover the Story.

Second exodus. Seventy years after they were exiled, the people of God were allowed to return home. In some ways, it felt like a second exodus (Jer 16:14-15). As in the first exodus, the people have another chance to really live out the ideals of the wilderness experience. And to a certain extent, things are better. Sabbath and other aspects of worshiping God take on greater meaning. People study Torah, God's law.

In several ways, however, they fell short. Worshiping God through right living continued to be a challenge (Isa 58), and there was an ongoing need to learn to trust God for everything. Perhaps their greatest dilemma was deciding how to be the chosen people who would bless others. Back in Jerusalem, the small percentage of Jews who were not exiled had intermarried with other peoples. When the exiled Jews return to Judah, they have to decide what to do about the foreign spouses and children. Ezra leads a reform, calling for all Jews to get rid of the foreigners.

On one hand, Ezra is concerned for purity (Ezra 9:1-4). Some parts of the law actually forbade the marrying of foreigners (Exod 34:15-16; Deut 7:3-4), and he really wants to obey God. That concern for honoring God is something we can admire. On the other hand, Ezra excludes people from worshiping God just because of their bloodline. He seems to forget moments when foreigners were included in the story—including many slaves, who came out of Egypt with the Israelites, and non-Israelite women, Rahab and Ruth, who married Israelites and became ancestors of the kings. He forgets what

Finding the Book —H. Copping

Tara: So what Ezra did was wrong?

Mike: We have to remember that God loves all people. It's whether you obey or not that is important.

Tara: But wasn't there a real threat that foreign people might tempt them to worship other gods and break their covenant with God? Aren't there verses in Exodus that say, "Don't marry foreign people"?

Josh: But don't forget the story of Ruth. The foreigner in that story, Ruth, was the hero, and she married an Israelite.

Luke: Here's the question again. What if I were one of the foreign wives who had to leave? It doesn't seem fair. I just wish the Bible would give us more of a sense of what God was doing with everyone else during this time.

Michele: There is so much tension between the call not to conform to the world and our call to be in the world as witnesses. This story shows us that tension without necessarily resolving it.

Abraham and all his descendants were chosen to do—to bless every family on earth (Gen 12:3).

That's how the Old Testament Story ends—with many of these struggles remaining and many questions unresolved. But look at the ground we've covered: God's people broke their part of the covenant many times. They forgot the vision of the wilderness. They mixed the worship of God with other religions. Yet God remained faithful. God sent judges and, later on, prophets. God worked with less than perfect situations, such as the monarchy. When the people truly got desperate, God rescued them. And even God's judgment on them—their loss of independence as other nations took them over—became a blessing in disguise.

After the exile, the people of God started yearning more and more for a new kind of leader, a leader who would finally help them stay completely faithful to God. They called this leader the Messiah, or "the anointed one." Sometimes they proclaimed a human as a messiah, such as the Persian king Cyrus, when he defeated Babylon and allowed the Jews to return to their homeland (Isa 45:1). At other times, they looked forward to a time when God would send someone special who would be the final Messiah (Isa 42, 49, and 61). When would he come? What would he be like?

That's what the next chapter is about.

Summing it up:

- **God has an ultimate plan but stays with us when we choose the wrong way.** God gives us free choice, and sometimes we make choices that show a lack of faith (like the Israelites turning back from Canaan the first time or choosing a king). Such choices bring painful consequences, but "judgment" calls us to better things.

- **God sends people to help us be faithful.** In the Bible, God sends judges and prophets to remind the people of God's way. The message was often unpopular, but when the people of God listened, things got a lot better.

- **Syncretism, the mixing of two religions, can be deadly to our faith.** The Israelites were tempted to worship both Yahweh and idols just to be on the safe side. We also can compromise our faith by mixing it with values of our culture. At the same time, God calls us to love and welcome others.

- **God is with us even in the darkest of times.** When the people of Judah and Israel went into exile, it really felt like the bottom had dropped out of their world. But God was there. God uses painful experiences to bring us back to where we should be.

- **How we see the Bible helps determine how we view Jesus and understand our lives as Christians.** These God-inspired stories in the Bible tell what did happen, not necessarily what should have happened. From the whole mix, we must figure out who God really is and how to be faithful to God.

a **spiritual discipline** to practice:

There are many things in our lives that ask for our ultimate trust. A big part of being a Christian is to dare to trust God over everything else. Take some time to think about what you are tempted to trust instead of trusting God when times get tough for you. Write out a list of these things. Do you ever mix "gods" or, in other words, do you say you trust in God but you also rely on _____, just in case?

After reflecting on your "baals," write a letter to God. Will you ask for forgiveness, for help to trust God more, to see God's power more, or maybe all of the above? What will you write?

Topics in chapter 4

- **God comes in human form**
- **Jesus: a different kind of messiah**
- **Jubilee living from the heart**
- **Good news for all, even enemies**
- **Words, actions, and salvation**
- **A call to follow**

Story line:
Jesus is born
Jesus' work of healing and teaching

4. Enter Jesus

Everyone in first-century Palestine wanted a messiah—someone God would send to deliver the people from their oppression. The Roman Empire was brutal. Many people were taxed to the point of starvation. Some sold themselves or their children into slavery. Troublemakers were crucified. When the Romans said, "Jump!" the Jews asked, "How high?" This was the world Jesus was born into—politically charged, the streets unsafe, lots of poor people. The future looked bleak.

The Jews remembered the exodus; they longed again for deliverance. Some Jews longed for a military solution, and others longed for another Moses who would promote such radical obedience that God would surely rescue them. But all wanted the same thing: to get rid of the Romans.

Humble birth, lousy location . . . Jesus was born to a carpenter and his wife, natives of the northern region of Galilee. They gave him a name that was as common as Bob, and after his birth in Bethlehem they lived in the equivalent of Newark, New Jersey, or Tofield, Alberta. No government parade on the day of his arrival. No religious escort to the temple. Jesus was born in a stable because there was no room in the inn. And rumors floated through the village that he was an illegitimate child. Jesus had very humble beginnings (Matt 1:18-25; Luke 2; Mark 6:3).

I used to think about Jesus as just a good teacher. That's okay as far as it goes, but it's like condemning Jesus with faint praise. He's the best teacher. But he's more than that. You can't dismiss the miracles or the way he was God. I don't want just a good teacher; I want someone who can change my life. —*Mike*

Yahweh saves

Josh: They named him Bob? Isn't that disrespectful?

Michele: I don't mean to be. Of all the names in the world, Jesus is perfect because it means "Yahweh [the Lord] saves." And because of who Jesus is, that name has such special meaning.

On the other hand, many other little boys were called Yeshua (Jesus), too. As a human, Jesus experienced everything that we have experienced (Heb 4:15). See, this is the incarnation. Totally God, but at the same time totally human, even to the point of getting a common name.

Luke: Why this story of the virgin birth?

Michele: Matthew and Luke had no good motive for including the story—unless it was true. The pagan religions of that day had similar stories—god-heroes born of a woman who was impregnated by a god. Why would the Christians have risked including this similarity to paganism unless it was true and supported their message that Jesus was the Son of God?

Tara: You just can't have a faith without accepting some beliefs that can't be explained completely. The point is—do you choose to believe in a God who does supernatural things or not?

. . . but extraordinary life. In as many ways as Jesus' birth was common, it was also uncommon. He was conceived supernaturally in the womb of a virgin (Luke 1:26-38). Royal astrologers from the East came to pay him homage (Matt 2:1-12). So did shepherds, people considered too unclean to worship in the synagogue because of their occupation (Luke 2:8-20). In some ways Jesus was totally unknown, but in other ways he was known too well. Herod wanted to kill him so much that he had all the infant boys in Bethlehem slaughtered (Matt 2:16-18).

Jesus: a life outside the box

What Jesus does for the next 30 years, except for his trip to the temple at age 12 (Luke 2:41-52), is left out of the Gospel accounts. The Gospels pick up the story when the adult Jesus asks his cousin John to baptize him (Luke 3:21-22). John is calling the Jews to repent—to turn around and change their sinful behaviors and attitudes. Jesus didn't sin (Heb 4:15), yet he too asks for baptism. Why? Surely Jesus wanted to be an example for the people then and for us today, but perhaps something more was going on.

incarnation: the belief that God took on human form in Jesus Christ

As John baptizes Jesus, a voice speaks from heaven: "You are my Son, the Beloved; with you I am well pleased" (Luke 3:22). The quote contains two fragments of Scripture that had special meaning for the Jews. "You are my Son, the Beloved" comes from Psalm 2, which was used whenever a king was enthroned as the new ruler. "With you I am well pleased" is a part of Isaiah's prophecy about a suffering servant (Isa 42:1). Put together, these quotes send a message to Jesus and to the crowd about who Jesus is. Jesus is a king, a servant king (Luke 3:21-22).

What kind of messiah? Jesus has to reflect on what God is calling him to do as Messiah. So he heads for the wilderness for 40 days (Luke 4:1-13). There, Satan (or "the devil") offers ideas about what kind of king Jesus can be. Satan gives Jesus three offers. The first is to satisfy his hunger by turning rocks into bread. After all, Jesus hasn't eaten in 40 days. Satan then offers him all the political power in the world if he will just bow down and worship the devil. Finally, Satan takes Jesus to the top of the temple. There Satan reminds him that angels will not let him be hurt, and he can prove that by jumping off the pinnacle.

What could hurt? What's wrong with turning rocks into bread? Didn't Jesus do something similar when he fed the 5,000

If you only see Jesus as God, then his death on the cross probably doesn't mean much, because he wouldn't have felt any pain. And you downplay all his ethical teachings and focus only on the miracles. But if you only see Jesus as human, then you downplay Jesus' miracles and especially his resurrection. But it blows my mind to think he's both God and human. —*Josh*

(Luke 9:10-17)? If he had political and military power he could "gently persuade" the whole world to worship God. And what a great idea to demonstrate God's power by jumping off the temple roof! That would impress people.

No, the temptations—especially turning rocks into bread—were not so terrible in themselves. The larger issue at stake was what kind of messiah Jesus would be. Forcing people in any way—either by economic incentives, military power, or by wowing them with miracles—was not God's way.

There were times when Jesus did these very things. He fed 5,000 with five loaves and two fish (Luke 9:10-17). He did many miracles. But he often told people who were healed not to broadcast the news of their healing (Mark 3:7-12). He refused to do miracles when people wanted "proof" of his power (see Mark 8:11-12). Jesus knew that if he became an economic, wonder-working, or military messiah that the people would not follow him out of love. He also knew that if he became any of these messiahs, he could avoid what he knew lay ahead of him, what lies ahead for anyone who follows God fully. He could avoid suffering. He could avoid the cross. That was the real temptation.

But to that temptation, Jesus says no. He says no to tricking or forcing people to follow him. He says no to the easy way. And in doing so, he says yes to suffering.

Jubilee for everyone. Having decided what kind of messiah he would not be, Jesus now has to announce what kind of messiah he will be. He heads for Nazareth, the town where he had grown up (Luke 4:16-30). There, at a synagogue service, he reads from the scroll of Isaiah. "The Spirit of the Lord is upon me, because he has anointed me to bring good news to the poor. He has sent me to proclaim release to the captives and recovery of sight to the blind, to let the

Temptation isn't sin in itself. It's saying yes to temptation that's wrong. Many new Christians struggle with this. They think they're terrible and displeasing to God because they have all these temptations in their minds. But everyone has temptations. The problem comes when we yield to them.
—*Rosella*

oppressed go free, to proclaim the year of the Lord's favor" (Luke 4:18-19).

When he sits down, every eye is fixed on him. "Today this scripture has been fulfilled in your hearing," he says (Luke 4:21). Now they are really amazed. Isn't this Joseph's son from down the street? But there is something in his voice that gives them the feeling that the Jubilee he read about would soon be theirs. They have been longing for these very prophecies to come true. This is wonderful news.

Jesus takes this good news a step further. He speaks of the prophets helping Gentiles, like the widow of Zarephath (1 Kings 17:8-24) and Naaman the Syrian (2 Kings 5:1-19). This good news—freedom for the captives, sight for the blind, food for the poor—is God's desire for non-Israelites as well as Israelites. This good news, Jesus was saying, is not only for the Jews. God has always intended it for every person, every people, every race.

Living it out

The good news that Jesus was sharing in the temple (Luke 4:18-19) still shakes people up. Many of the members of the church I attend got to know Jesus while they were in a pretty bad place: alcoholism, abuse, broken families. They're already on the margins because many are undocumented immigrants. Many people, even Christians, would say they're living the consequences of their choices.

But these folks are living examples of the fact that we don't have to be perfect for God to start working on us. After seeing in their own lives that Jesus' good news is for everyone, they're the most willing to share it. Our church is a place where together we carry pain, face fears, and rely on God's grace. Just like the widow of Zarephath wanted to announce Elijah's holiness after her son was healed (1 Kings 17:24), my brothers and sisters want to announce how God brings order, peace, and joy to their lives today. They're happy to spread the news to everyone, because as outsiders, they have been welcomed in and changed by Jesus' story. *—Maria C. M. Byler, Philadelphia, Pennsylvania*

Now they want to kill him. The people who admired him only moments before become so angry they try to hurl him off a cliff. The wonderful hometown boy is suddenly a threat. Jesus dares to contradict their treasured belief that they are God's favorite people? Jesus dares to break down the ethnic boundary they have tried to put around God? This is unthinkable!

Do some of Jesus' teachings make you mad, like the people of Nazareth who wanted to throw Jesus off the cliff? If you say no, is that because you don't think you have to follow the teachings that seem difficult or scary to do? What would Jesus say to you today? Can Jesus help you follow him even when it's difficult or scary?

"Gentle Jesus, meek and mild" —is that really how it is? When Jesus healed a man in the synagogue and the Pharisees opposed him, Jesus looked on them "with anger; . . . grieved at their hardness of heart" (Mark 3:5). Then there was the temple scene (Matt 21:12-13). Jesus had feelings. He was brave enough to stand up to people. He knew when to be gentle, and he knew when to let them have it.
—*Rosella's journal*

Sermon on Mount —F. Hoffmann

Good news for the whole person. The very things Jesus read at the synagogue in Nazareth, he made into reality.

- Jesus healed physical diseases.

- He spoke against economic injustice and told the rich to share their wealth (Luke 18–19). He brought the "year of Jubilee" (see page 42) to people from all walks of life (Luke 7:18-23).

- Jesus brought understanding for the heart and healing for the soul (John 3–4; Luke 10:38-41).

- He helped people find forgiveness (Mark 2:1-12).

- He cast out demons (Luke 4:31-37).

- He freed people from the destructive power of sin. He condemned sin and at the same time loved the sinner (John 8:1-11).

Like God at the time of the exodus, Jesus saw oppression of all kinds, and he delivered people from that oppression.

Loving the enemy. One such person who needed to be set free was a young lawyer, who asks Jesus what he must do to inherit eternal life. Jesus recites for him the great commandment from the Law: "You shall love the Lord your God with all your heart, and with all your soul, and with all your strength, and with all your mind; and your neighbor as yourself. . . . do this, and you will live (Luke 10:25-28; see also Deut 6:4-5) But wanting to justify himself, the lawyer asks, "Well, who is my neighbor?"

So Jesus tells a parable. Three people see a wounded man lying on the road. The first and second ones are religious men, a priest and a Levite. They don't stop to help the dying man, probably so they won't defile themselves and ruin their chances to do religious duties at the

Are the life and teachings of **Jesus** just as important to you as his death and resurrection? What does it mean that Jesus is one hundred percent human and one hundred percent divine? How does that perspective affect your faith and life?

temple. A third man also comes by—a Samaritan. He stops and helps the wounded man, even going so far as to pay for him to have special care at an inn (Luke 10:25-37).

The story looks innocent enough until we realize that Samaritans were despised people, considered by the Jews of the time to be filthy lowlifes because of their mixed ancestry. But it was the unacceptable Samaritan who was the obvious hero of Jesus' story, the one who truly loved his neighbor. Jesus wanted the young lawyer to see that godliness was more than obeying God's rules and regulations. He wanted to free the lawyer from the oppression of his own prejudice. He wanted him to be able to see God, even in those whom society rejected.

The Prodigal Son —A. Birkle

Forgiveness. But what happens when the lawyer—or we as Christians—can't meet such high standards? In another parable, Jesus tells of two sons: the young one who runs off with his share of the inheritance and the older one who stays home as he should. After burning his money on riotous living, the younger son faces starvation. Coming to his senses, he decides to go home to beg forgiveness and at least try to work as a slave for his father. All this time, the father has been watching for him, longing for him, loving him just as much as he loves the older son. So when the boy gets within sight, the father runs out to greet him, forgiving him before the words "I'm sorry" can tumble out of his mouth (Luke 15:11-32).

We are all like the boy who ran off. We sin, we screw up, we are unable to love the despised Samaritans in our town. And God watches out

Mike: Okay, but what about the older son? Finish the story.

Michele: He was green with envy when the father threw a huge "welcome home" party for his undeserving brother.

Mike: I can see why he'd be mad if he had never gotten a party.

Luke: Who said he never got a party—maybe he just didn't go to the parties that were really meant for him all along.

Rosella: It's hard for people who have never rebelled in a big way to understand God's grace. They forget that they need it, too.

the window every day, looking for us. When we start to "come home," God races out and embraces us with love.

Good news: living from the heart

Jesus truly brought good news for everyone. This is especially clear in the Sermon on the Mount (Matt 5–7). In many ways, this collection of teachings mirrors the high ideals that God gave the Israelites in the wilderness. Jesus calls his followers to love their enemies (5:43-48), pray with true motives (6:5-15), and give up worrying over what they will eat or wear (6:25-34).

Religious leaders made many extra rules to make sure that, at least on the outside, they were obeying God's laws. Jesus cut to the heart of the matter. Jesus addressed attitudes. Those who refrain from murder but still hate in their hearts are as bad as murderers (5:21-26). Those who have lust in their hearts are as bad as those who commit adultery (5:27-30). In one powerful hyperbole (exaggerated example), Jesus suggests that people cut off their hands and gouge out their eyes if doing so will help them change their ways (5:29-30). People need a change of heart—and that goes even deeper than changing or losing our limbs! Jesus was trying to get at the root of ethical choices, which literally is what the word *radical* suggests.

The Beatitudes

Jesus' Sermon on the Mount (Matt 5–7) is one of the most quoted summaries of Jesus' radical teaching about how one lives under God's reign. It begins with a statement about what makes people truly happy in life:

Blessed are the poor in spirit, for theirs is the kingdom of heaven.

Blessed are those who mourn, for they will be comforted.

Blessed are the meek, for they will inherit the earth.

Blessed are those who hunger and thirst for righteousness, for they will be filled.

Blessed are the merciful, for they will receive mercy.

Blessed are the pure in heart, for they will see God.

Blessed are the peacemakers, for they will be called children of God.

Blessed are those who are persecuted for righteousness' sake, for theirs is the kingdom of heaven.

Blessed are you when people revile you and persecute you and utter all kinds of evil against you falsely on my account. Rejoice and be glad, for your reward is great in heaven, for in the same way they persecuted the prophets who were before you.

—Matthew 5:3-12

Luke: The Sermon on the Mount sounds like an impossible standard to live by.

Rosella: But there's grace, too! The Lord says that all our needs will be met. If God clothes the lilies of the field, which are here today and gone tomorrow, won't God take care of us?

Luke: Even when it comes to living out these really hard standards?

Tara: Nothing is impossible with God. And what is the only thing that can give us the strength to do the impossible calling of the sermon? Not cutting off arms. Only the strength of Jesus and his love.

Beyond words and actions. What does it mean to follow Jesus? What is involved in being a Christian? Jesus said a lot of things that can be hard to figure out. In John 3, he tells Nicodemus he has to be "born again" (John 3:1-8). A rich young ruler asks Jesus straight up, "What must I do to inherit eternal life?" Jesus tells him to sell all his possessions and give the money to the poor (Luke 18:18-30). According to the Sermon on the Mount, one becomes a child of God by loving enemies (Matt 5:44-45). Other times Jesus simply tells people, "Follow me" (Mark 1:17).

The early church expressed salvation somewhat differently. In Acts 2:38, the apostle Peter urges the crowd to "Repent, and be baptized every one of you in the name of Jesus Christ so that your sins may be forgiven; and you will receive the gift of the Holy Spirit." Paul writes in Romans 10:9 that if you "confess with your lips that Jesus is Lord and believe in your heart that God raised him from the dead, you will be saved." How do you understand all these things put together?

Different ways to say "I'm a Christian."

I'm a believer in Jesus.

I'm a follower of Christ.

I have a relationship with Jesus.

I'm born again.

I'm saved.

I have surrendered my life to Christ.

I have accepted Jesus as my Savior and Lord.

On one hand, it's not a big deal how you say it. These are different ways of saying the same thing. On the other hand, each way has a certain emphasis. If you really stress that you're a "follower," you might start to emphasize outer obedience to God more than the grace and spiritual transformation that are part of being a Christian. If you stress that you are "saved," you might begin to think Christianity is only about a conversion event that secures you a place in heaven someday. Being a Christian involves an event and a process. God reaches out to us and we respond—and keep responding. It's simple, yet it's a mystery.

Perhaps the Sermon on the Mount can help us understand. In Matthew 7:21, Jesus says, "Not everyone who says to me, 'Lord, Lord,' will enter the kingdom of heaven, but only the one who does the will of my Father in heaven." At first glance, this statement cautions us against just saying the right words or simply agreeing to a set of statements. It's got to be deeper than that.

It also goes deeper than actions. Jesus continues, "On that day many will say to me, 'Lord, Lord, did we not prophesy in your name, and cast out demons in your name, and do many deeds of power in your name?' Then I will declare to them, 'I never knew you; go away from me, you evildoers'" (Matt 7:21-23). Not only does our salvation need to be deeper than saying the right words, it also has to be more than outward actions, even spectacular acts of faith.

Both words and actions can fake the real thing. But what is the real thing? Salvation is rich enough and mysterious enough that different people use different ways to explain it. But real salvation always means a change in us. Like Nicodemus, we are "born again." We act differently because we have experienced an inner change. Part of salvation is asking God to forgive us our sins and to heal the relationship with God that sin has destroyed. We also allow God to transform us so that all our relationships are restored. We confess that Jesus is our Lord not because saying those words will save us, but because we serve a different master than the rest of the world does. We live lives that please God not because we have to in order to become or remain Christians, but because that's who we are. We have a new identity.

What do people today need to be saved from—spiritually, physically, and emotionally? How would Jesus meet people's deepest needs if he were worshiping and living today?

Salvation: done deal, or in process?

Mike: Back up. If salvation means all our relationships are restored, I'm in trouble.

Michele: I see your point. We are saved *in* our brokenness as much as *out of* our brokenness.

Tara: So if some of my relationships with people are not good, I'm still okay?

Michele: It's another paradox. We experience salvation as we say yes to Jesus (Eph 2:8), but we also "work out" that salvation in our lives (Phil 2:12; 1 Cor 1:18). We also look forward to the day when our salvation will be complete (Rom 8:18-23). When we don't feel like loving our enemies or feeding the hungry, it doesn't mean we're not Christians anymore. It means that God is still in process with us.

Making it personal

The disciples were mystified over who their rabbi was. Like their fellow Jews, they were expecting a different type of messiah. Why didn't Jesus get rid of the Romans by force? Why didn't he let people proclaim him as Messiah, especially after one of his miraculous healings? And why did he count prostitutes, Roman soldiers, tax collectors, and Samaritans among his friends? To add to the confusion, Jesus talked about his own upcoming suffering and death.

Jesus knew about their confusion. So one day he asks them, "Who do people say that the Son of Man is?" They answer, "Some say John the Baptist, but others Elijah, and still others Jeremiah or one of the prophets." Then he asks them, "But who do you say that I am?" Simon Peter replies, "You are the Messiah, the Son of the living God." Jesus is pleased with his answer and says, "You are Peter [literally Rock], and on this rock I will build my church, and the gates of Hades will not prevail against it" (Matt 16:13-18).

Jesus then tells them what it means for him to be the Messiah (Matt 16:21-28). This is the hardest thing for the disciples to understand. It means refusing to compromise one's obedience to God. It means saying no to violence and yes to suffering love. For Jesus, it means death. For many of the disciples, it will mean death, too.

Peter is so shocked at Jesus' words that he scolds him. How can the Messiah allow himself to suffer and die? And what does Jesus mean by rising again in three days? But Jesus retorts, "Get behind me, Satan!" Jesus' temptation in the wilderness has snuck back in: Peter is suggesting that he avoid the cross.

I think that by our lives, every day, we say to the world who we really think Jesus is.
—*Rosella*

Who do you say Jesus is? Who does your life say Jesus is?

Charge to Peter —Raphael

What about us? As we reflect on who Jesus is and hear the good news of Jesus and his love, we have to respond in some way. It's not enough to know about Jesus and salvation. It's not enough to be able to explain what everything means in the Story and how it all fits together. Knowing all this, you must make a choice. Will you follow Jesus? Will you accept God's great love for you, trusting in this love and letting that transform your life? Will you say yes to him? Will you let Jesus change every aspect of your life—beginning now?

Summing it up:

The Story so far: From the beginning, God communicated with humans through the Law and prophets, through the written stories of God's dealings with the Israelites, and through direct encounters with people. It was good stuff, but the people got the message all twisted around. *They interpreted God's message to fit their own needs.* Through Jesus, God took on human form and lived among us, experiencing with us the pains, frustrations, and joys of being human. (He died and he rose again, too, but that's the next chapter.) In doing so, he showed us the true nature and will of God. Through Jesus, we have a glimpse of God (John 1:1-14, 18; Heb 1:1-3). What wonderful news!

- **Jesus is fully God and fully human.** We take by faith that Jesus is one hundred percent God and one hundred percent human. If we overstress the humanity of Jesus, we take his ethics seriously but can only see him as a good moral teacher. If we overstress the divinity of Christ, we get excited about what Christ can do for us spiritually, but we tend to ignore his teachings about what is right and wrong.

What does it mean to "follow" Jesus? What differences and similarities are there between the way the 12 disciples followed Jesus and the way we follow him today?

They say a picture is worth a thousand words, but an experience is worth a thousand pictures.

- **Jesus chose to be a servant.** Jesus made a deliberate choice to be the kind of messiah that would not use military force. Instead he would defeat evil through obedient love for God. This was—and is—the highest and most powerful form of power. We are called to make that same choice today.

- **Through Jesus, God offered salvation to everyone.** Jesus brought freedom from oppression of all kinds—physical, social, and spiritual. To emphasize one over others distorts the true meaning of salvation.

- **Jesus calls people to follow him. Jesus didn't only heal people and teach the crowds.** He gathered a group of disciples and trained them to do his work. We too are called into a journey with Jesus.

a **spiritual discipline** to practice:

Reread the story of the prodigal son, found in Luke 15:11-32. Now, place yourself in the shoes of the younger son and imagine that God, like the loving father, wants to write you a love letter. Write down what you hear inside you.

Now place yourself in the shoes of the older son and imagine that God, like the loving father, wants to write you a love letter. Write down what you hear inside.

Topics in chapter 5

- **Jesus: a threat to the powers that be**
- **Love, service, sacrifice**
- **Why Jesus died**
- **And what it has to do with us**
- **Why Jesus rose again**
- **And why it matters**

Story line:
The Last Supper
Jesus washes the disciples' feet
Jesus' trial and crucifixion
Jesus' resurrection

5. Mission Accomplished

In some ways, things looked the same as Jesus finished his work in Galilee and "set his face" toward Jerusalem (Luke 9:53). He still healed the sick and he still taught the people with an authority they had never before encountered, but now Jesus seems more determined. There is a look in his eyes. He talks about rejection and suffering (Luke 9:21-22). He tells the disciples that they too must bear their crosses, they too must be willing to suffer for the sake of God and others (Luke 9:23-26). Even though foxes have holes to sleep in and birds have nests to rest in, Jesus says, they will have no house to go home to (Luke 9:57-62). He talks about his own upcoming death.

Jesus' life was so awesome. But his death and resurrection—words can't describe what all that means to me.
—*Tara*

What does it mean to bear a cross?

Tara: To hear some people, it's like when they get allergies, they have a "cross" to bear. "Well, that's just my cross to bear."

Luke: Jesus isn't talking about just any kind of suffering, is he?

Mike: He's talking about being willing to suffer for following him.

Josh: But the scary thing in my life is that no one is persecuting me for being a Christian. What does that say about me?

Confrontation: Jesus' last hours

All this suffering and death talk was hard for his followers to comprehend on the day Jesus rode into Jerusalem. The crowds loved him. It was Passover, the sacred festival that celebrated the time God liberated the Israelites from slavery in Egypt. The streets were full. Passover always raised Jewish hopes that maybe this year the Messiah would come. As Jesus' procession comes near the city, the people shout, "Hosanna!" (Lord, save!) and put their cloaks and palm branches on the ground to form a carpet for the donkey to walk on (Luke 19:28-40). Is this the one who will free them from the Romans?

As much as the common folk loved Jesus, however, the religious leaders feared and hated him. What Jesus does at the temple that next day only confirms those fears. Jesus sees moneychangers and merchants doing business in the temple—and he is infuriated. They were most likely overcharging folks, but perhaps more than anything else, Jesus is angry that this noisy marketplace is set up in the very spot reserved for non-Jews to pray and worship. In his anger, he overturns the tables and sets the livestock free. The merchants and moneychangers run in every direction. Jesus says, "My house shall be called a house of prayer for all the nations. But you have made it a den of robbers" (Mark 11:15-17; see also John 2:13-22).

What was behind Jesus' action in the temple (Mark 11:15-17)? Does this story justify the use of violence to defeat evil? Why, or why not?

Michele: So what do you think? Is this action out of character with the rest of Jesus?

Tara: He was angry. He was radical. I think that's okay.

Rosella: People can use this story to support their own use of violence. "See, Jesus did it, so we can, too."

Mike: I heard someone once say that if people want to fight wars by knocking tables over, go for it. I agree. Those kinds of wars aren't going to hurt anybody.

The temple leaders were furious. Jesus was already a threat to their way of life. He healed on the Sabbath. He talked with Gentiles, Samaritans, and prostitutes. He told the crowds that their righteousness must go beyond the righteousness of the religious leaders, the scribes, and Pharisees. And the common people loved Jesus. They hung on his every word. Now the riot in the temple is more than these leaders can tolerate. So they begin to plot a way to get rid of him (Luke 22:1-2).

The Last Supper. That Thursday, Jesus gathers with his disciples to celebrate the Passover meal. At Passover each Jewish family reenacted the night when God liberated the slaves in Egypt (see pages 30–35). In the original Passover, they were instructed to prepare lamb and herbs and smear the blood of an unblemished lamb on the doorposts. They ate standing up, ready to leave Egypt at a moment's notice. It was a tense night. The angel of death passed over every house that had the lamb's blood on the door. Where there was no blood, the eldest son was killed (Exod 12:29-32, 43-49).

Jesus as Lamb

Tara: Okay, this is getting back to the exodus as a picture of our salvation, right? The perfect lamb is like Jesus, and all the slaves had to do was put the blood over their door and the death angel would pass over them. I think this is so cool.

Josh: And crossing the Red Sea is like baptism?

Tara: Yes.

Josh: And the Promised Land is . . . heaven?

Tara: I guess.

Michele: This is one picture of salvation and there are others. But when Jesus and his friends shared the Passover meal, Jesus gave the traditional elements, bread and wine, a new meaning. He broke the bread and said, "Take and eat. This is my body." He took the cup of wine and said, "Drink, this is my blood." Jesus was honoring the old covenant that God made with the people, and at the same time he was initiating a new covenant. He was thinking ahead to the shedding of his own blood (Luke 22:14-23).

(See pages 165–166 for more on Jesus as the "Lamb who was slain" and page 47 for more on covenants.)

The Lord's Supper (communion)

Josh: We do it to remember the death of Jesus.

Luke: It helps us look forward to the big banquet of God's kingdom in the future.

Tara: The Lord's Supper also builds unity in local groups of believers.

Michele: The apostle Paul told the Corinthian believers that if they didn't love and care for each other they would totally miss the meaning of the Lord's Supper. They would eat and drink in ways that dishonored Christ (see 1 Cor 11:17-34).

Luke: So in one way, the Lord's Supper is about the mysterious presence of Jesus right there with you. But in another way, Christ's presence among us depends on something as ordinary as caring for each other as church.

Rosella: So, do we drop the Old Testament meaning of exodus, or don't we celebrate that, too?

Michele: Can't it be all those things?

See the Confession of Faith summary of Article 12 about communion on page 175.

What connection does the Last Supper and Jesus' washing of his disciples' feet have with the meaning of Jesus' death and resurrection?

Will you let me be your servant? If the minds of the disciples weren't boggled yet, they would be soon. Their mouths hung open. The Master, their beloved Teacher, puts on a servant's apron and kneels down with a basin of water right before their eyes (John 13:1-20). Surely not, they think, surely the Master will not wash their feet; that is servants' work! Yet as he takes the first mud-caked foot, they knew that yes, this is what he means to do. Peter cringes at the idea. "You shall never wash my feet!" Jesus smiles a weary smile. He knows that before Peter—or any of them, for that matter—can be the humble servant leaders they have been called to be, they must first receive that same gentle love.

Betrayed . . . Jesus startles his friends yet again by announcing that one of them will betray him. All are in shock—except Judas, who had already struck a deal with the enemies of Jesus to turn him over. Judas may have gotten the wrong idea when Jesus cleared out the temple. Maybe he thought that now, especially if forced into the situation,

Living it out

Each first Sunday of the month, those who gather for worship at First Mennonite Church of Iowa City remember Christ's body and blood offered for all as we celebrate communion. It enables us to see how God's story becomes our story through the lens of Jesus' life, death, and resurrection. It invites us to understand what God has done and what God is doing in the world, as an expression of Christ's self-giving, nonviolent love that is more powerful than death.

As each person receives the bread, they hear their name: "Jane, the body of Christ broken for you." And as they receive the juice, they hear, "Larry, receive the love of Jesus." The celebration reminds us that Jesus' death and resurrection are at once of cosmic significance and very personal; we are reenacting an event of history; and we are participating now in God's kingdom coming to this earth, this community, this person.

On Maundy Thursday, we include footwashing. This is a more intimate service of remembering Jesus' servant love for his disciples. It is a time of confessing the sin that clings to us, hindering our relationships with God and others. And it is a time of celebrating God's cleansing forgiveness offered in the humble, gentle act of daring to touch and care for one another's (potentially stinky) feet!

I believe it is a powerful and appropriate way to consider with our bodies as well as our minds how radically humble and loving was Jesus' upside-down way of living and dying. —*Karla Stoltzfus Detweiler, Iowa City, Iowa*

Jesus would fight the Romans with his supernatural power. Perhaps Judas thought he could be the one to give Jesus the incentive he needed. In any case, Jesus now tells Judas, "Do quickly what you are going to do" (John 13:27). And Judas walks out the door to find the religious leaders.

The rest of the group trudges to the Garden of Gethsemane. Realizing what lies ahead, Jesus needs time to pray. He is in agony. Being fully human, he dreads the pain of torture and death and

Michele: Some Christian groups, including some Mennonites, practice a ceremony of footwashing, often in the same service as communion. In pairs, people take turns kneeling down to wash each other's feet in a basin as Jesus instructed his disciples to do (John 13:14). What do you think of that practice?

Josh: It's not been my experience much, so I'm pretty uncomfortable with it.

Luke: It's not like it, or any other ritual for that matter, brings you salvation. When I do it, I feel queasy at the time, too. But when I wash feet, something happens to me. It helps break me open to loving the person I'm footwashing with.

Tara: Washing feet means—every day—being a servant to everyone you meet. But especially to people who drive you crazy. It's not just doing nice things for them. It's living in such a way that you really do care about them, and you serve them for their sakes not yours.

Rosella: It even means you let them serve you.

See the Confession of Faith summary of Article 13 about footwashing on page 175.

shrinks from the coming humiliation. And so, in this late hour, he asks God to take away this "cup" of suffering if possible (Mark 14:32-36). The temptations from the wilderness loom once again in front of him. He must have wondered, Is there any other way?

Yet he knew the answer. The only way to avoid suffering was to take matters into his own hands, to somehow force the people to follow him through military might, economic incentives, or through a never-ending parade of miracles. To go any other way than faithful obedience to God would be to compromise that obedience. Yet to obey, he knew, would be to die. "Not what I want, but what you want," he finally prays, fully committing himself to God.

Arrested . . . Jesus' decision comes none too soon, for Judas is already in the garden, leading the temple guards and soldiers to arrest him. Peter pulls a sword and takes a swing at the nearest enemy, cutting off the ear of one of the servants. Surely, thinks Peter, if there ever was an appropriate time for violence, if there ever was a time when the ends justified the means, surely it is now when his master is in danger. But Jesus says no. If he needs protection, he explains, he can call thousands of angels for help. "All who take the sword, will perish by the sword," Jesus says (Matt 26:52). Jesus then heals the ear of his enemy (Luke 22:51).

Tried . . . After a long night of interrogation in a trial that made mockery of justice, Jesus stands before the Roman governor, Pilate. Pilate knows an innocent man when he sees one. He tries several times to set Jesus free. But Pilate himself is in a corner, for the religious leaders are blackmailing him. "If you release this man, you are no friend of the emperor . . . ," they said. "We have no king but the emperor" (John 19:12-15). Jesus' enemies wanted to get rid of Jesus so much that they were willing to compromise one of their most precious beliefs: the sovereignty of their own nation under God. In times past, the Jews risked death rather than pay allegiance to foreign rulers. Now these scribes and Pharisees hail Caesar as their king, because Jesus is that much of a threat.

The four gospels in the New Testament—Matthew, Mark, Luke, and John—each tell the story of Jesus slightly differently (see page 55). Especially here in the closing chapters, we see each gospel writer bringing out different details of the story. John, for example, does not tell about the Last Supper, but he does tell about Jesus washing the disciples' feet. In the story of the resurrection, Matthew has an angel greeting the women at the tomb; Luke tells of two men in dazzling white clothes; Mark has a "young man" at the tomb; John doesn't mention angels but has Jesus appearing to Mary.

For a rewarding Bible study challenge, compare the closing chapters of the gospels to discover what each author may have wanted to emphasize. For our discussion here, we draw details from all four stories, as you can see from the references in parentheses. But we recognize that trying to build a composite story does not do justice to each story.

Crucified . . . Reluctantly, Pilate sentences Jesus to be crucified, along with two others. It is a horrible ordeal. Jesus has already suffered from flogging, all night interrogations, and the emotional distress of knowing what lay ahead. Now, he will be put on a wooden cross, where his hands and feet will literally be nailed to the wood. Then, tearing his flesh even more, the whole cross will be hoisted into the ground. There, Jesus will hang, literally, with the weight of his own body causing immense pain with every breath.

Crucifixion was not only horribly painful, but also a public display of humiliation. The people come and mock Jesus. "He saved others; let him save himself if he is the Messiah . . . ." (Luke 23:35). If they only knew. By not saving himself, he is saving them.

Although the pain was almost unbearable, Jesus stayed conscious enough to speak and to take some control of this situation. He asks God to forgive the ones who crucified him (Luke 23:34). He offers forgiveness and comfort to the repentant man being crucified next to him (Luke 23:39-43). He cares for his mother in the midst of his own pain (John 19:26). Darkness falls over the area for three hours as Jesus wrestles with pain and the feeling of God's abandonment. Then with a loud cry, Jesus gives himself into God's care and dies (Luke 23:46). A Roman centurion gives a final testimony after Jesus dies. He says, "Surely this man was the Son of God" (Mark 15:39 NIV).

Tara: I don't think we can ever understand how painful the crucifixion was.

Josh: Maybe that's why some people want Jesus to be more divine than human, so they can believe that he somehow didn't suffer.

Mike: The wooden spikes in your wrists. The slow, agonizing death. Man, it's just so . . . hard to imagine.

Michele: No other religion has the cross and the resurrection. To worship a person who can't even get himself off a cross? To believe that Jesus can save you when it looks like he can't even save himself? It doesn't make sense until after the resurrection (see next chapter).

Why did Jesus have to die?

This has been an important question through the ages. How we answer that question helps determine how we understand God, our own relationship with God, and what it means to be a Christian.

First we have to remember why Jesus came. Did he come simply to die? Jesus so threatened the powers who were in control (see the discussion on the "powers," page 24) that those in authority killed him. If he only came to be a sacrifice for sin, then it would have been more merciful if he had just been killed as a baby. But Jesus also came to live and show us who God really is. And when he refused to budge on what he knew was the right thing to do, even when they threatened him with death, he defeated the evil that put him to death.

In simple language, we can say, Jesus loved you and me enough to come to earth to live and die, and because he did, we can know and love God. But the Bible says this in several different ways, some of which are outlined below. None of these ways of explaining why Jesus died should be taken by itself. Together they all help us understand this important concept.

1. Jesus' life and death is the perfect example of sacrificial, suffering love. Through his life, teaching, and death, Jesus showed us how to respond to evil—through nonviolence and enemy love. When we see the suffering and death of an innocent Jesus, we are morally revolted and take a hard look at our own violence and sin. We are called to experience God's salvation by reflecting similar sacrificial love in our own lives as disciples (1 Pet 2:21).

There is a weakness in this view. It's great to have the perfect example to follow. But is it enough? Is it enough to just reflect on the life of Jesus and then imitate that life? Or do we need a power greater than we are to truly conquer evil in a nonviolent way?

2. Jesus, through his death, paid for our sins. Another way to think about why Jesus died is to think about Jesus "dying" for our sins (1 Cor 15:3). Sometimes the Bible talks about humans becoming slaves to sin; the blood of Jesus is the ransom price that frees us (1 Pet 1:17–19). Sin can be like a money debt, that Jesus pays for us through his death (Rom 3:24). In the Old Testament times the people "atoned" for their sins by sacrificing pure lambs. In a sense, the animals took the punishment for sin, rather than the people. Jesus is called the Lamb of God (John 1:29).

Why did Jesus have to die? (continued)

But there are weaknesses in this view as well. Taken by itself, this view shows God as a God who demands someone's death (Jesus') in order to satisfy his honor or justice. What kind of a God is that? Second, it makes salvation from sin a purely spiritual matter that takes place outside of history, through an invisible transaction between God and Jesus. God's heart is changed, not ours. Our salvation has nothing to do with our way of life. This kind of "salvation" isn't concerned with the broken relationships we may have with others or the hold that sin or real-life oppression has in our lives.

3. Christ is the Victor. In this view, Jesus is in a cosmic battle where he defeats the powers of evil and death through a life lived in total, faithful obedience. This leads to death, and, ironically, it is in his death—when he looks the most helpless—that he defeats evil. How? When threatened and made to suffer horribly, Jesus does not retaliate. This exposes evil for what it really is, thus breaking its power. Then God raises Jesus from death, proving the victory that he, and all of us, can have over death (Col 2:15). We too have this resurrection power. Jesus' resurrection shows that there is a power greater than evil or force. In many ways, this view includes all the others but also emphasizes that humans are the ones to be changed, not God.

Of the three explanations of Jesus' death, which one means the most to you?

Here's another way to look at it. Jesus saved us not only by his death but also by his life, his teachings, his resurrection, and the coming of the Spirit. In all these ways, Jesus worked to heal one or more of the four broken relationships that sin destroys. Sin breaks our relationship with God. Jesus healed that relationship by offering forgiveness through the cross and also by showing us through his own life the incredible loving character of God! Sin breaks the relationship between us and other humans, and Jesus heals that relationship by showing ultimate love on the cross and by giving us the Spirit who can help us do the impossible—love our enemies. Sin breaks the relationship between us and our inner selves. Over and over Jesus took away people's shame by healing their bodies and forgiving their sins and loving them so that they could love themselves. Jesus still does that today. And the broken relationship we have with the physical world? Jesus takes care of that not only with his resurrection but also with his loving attention to the physical needs of people.

It's not that the cross isn't important to our salvation. It really is! But sometimes, when we fail to look at all of Jesus' life, we think only about the cross as payment for our sins, and then we settle for a salvation that only heals our broken relationship with God. That relationship is a very important one. But Jesus wants to provide a salvation for us that is more than a ticket to heaven. Jesus wants not only to forgive us, but also to restore us and transform us into the person who we were always meant to be. Jesus wants to heal every part of us.

All of these views are supported in the Bible, and like the Bible, we can embrace more than one explanation of why Jesus had to die. If taken alone, the second view can suggest that Jesus has no importance for how we live our lives, or that forgiveness of sins is the only part of salvation. In other words, salvation and human behavior are separated; salvation is only something that happens in the heavens. In the second and third views, Jesus also has meaning for how we live our lives. Our salvation heals not only our relationship with God, which sin broke, but also our relationship with ourselves, with others, and with all creation.

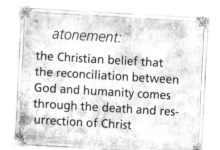

atonement: the Christian belief that the reconciliation between God and humanity comes through the death and resurrection of Christ

Tara: All of these things are important, I know, but you know what really hits me? Jesus loves me. Jesus loves me. That's what it's all about for me.

Rosella: I am a sinner; I was caught in a mess of sin, and Jesus brought me out. That's what I'm thankful for.

Mike: I think it's hard for some people to really believe God loves them. They have messed up so much, and I don't know, maybe salvation for them is just someone coming in and helping them get out of the mess.

Michele: But salvation is important for people whose lives aren't in a mess, too. You know, I wasn't in this big mess when I wanted to begin a relationship with Jesus. And guilt was kind of pushed on me, more than what I really felt myself. I knew I was supposed to feel bad about my life. I can feel guilty about not feeling guilty, you know? But for me, I wanted to know something, Someone. I just wanted God.

Buried . . . According to Jewish custom, dead bodies were to be removed from public view. With the Sabbath beginning the evening Jesus died, a secret follower of Jesus named Joseph of Arimathea moved quickly to honor the law. He asks permission to bury Jesus' body in a tomb he owns, and the authorities grant his request (Mark 15:42-47). As for Jesus' followers, most of whom had abandoned Jesus during his trial and crucifixion, the Sabbath itself was a dark day. They apparently hid in fear behind locked doors.

Raised to life . . . The events of early Sunday morning are told selectively in each of the gospel accounts (Matt 28:1-10; Mark 16:1-8; Luke 24:1-12; John 20:1-18). Early Sunday morning several women followers of Jesus set out early to finish the job of embalming Jesus' body. Grief filled their hearts, and worry, too. How would they move the heavy stone placed over the tomb? The Jewish leaders had requested the stone and guards to make sure no one stole the body. It would be impossible for these women to move it by themselves.

Jesus Appears to Mary —Correggio

But . . . what? The stone was rolled away! They couldn't believe their eyes! Did someone steal the body after all? They peek inside. The body is gone. Something terrible has happened. Someone took the body! Still in shock, they turn to see a bright light and . . . an angel? Jesus has risen from the dead, the angel says.

Going as fast as they can, they run to tell the others. The men are in shock and disbelief. As John tells it, Peter and John run to see for themselves that the tomb is empty (John 20:3). The grave-clothes lay by themselves. Perhaps? Can it be true? Is Jesus alive? It is too wonderful to be true!

Later, as Mary Magdalene lingers by the tomb, she meets a man. At first she thinks it is the gardener. But as he greets her by name, she realizes it is Jesus. She kneels at his feet in worship. At Jesus' bidding, Mary runs to tell the other disciples that she has seen the Lord.

In the next days and weeks, Jesus appears in various places and times to the disciples and others. In some ways, the body of Jesus is like their own bodies. He eats with them (Luke 24:42; John 21:9-14). He has the scars of crucifixion on his hands, feet, and side (Luke 24:39-40). In other ways, Jesus has a different kind of body. He can appear and disappear. He walks through locked doors (Luke 24:31, 36). Not only does the Spirit of Jesus interact with people, but the same body walks among the disciples, complete with the holes in his wrists and feet. His crucified body is different, and yet the same.

Why is Jesus' resurrection so important?

The resurrection was a central part of the Story as Jesus' followers told it (see Acts 2:29-36). It established that Jesus was indeed God's Son and the Messiah—Lord over all things, including the power of death. In his letter to the Corinthians, Paul writes that if Jesus didn't rise from the dead, their faith was useless (1 Cor 15:14). Christ's resurrection is a guarantee of our own resurrection as believers. We can praise God with Paul and say, "Death has been swallowed up in victory. . . . thanks be to God, who gives us the victory through our Lord Jesus Christ!" (1 Cor 15:54-57).

Imagine Christianity without the resurrection of Jesus. Do you think Christian faith would have survived without it?

The resurrection affects how we live. There were some people in the Corinthian church who thought that physical things, including our bodies, were useless, or at least inferior to the spiritual world (1 Cor 6:12-20; 1 Cor 15:35-58). So they reasoned that if their bodies were not going to be a part of their eternal life with God, then they could do anything they wanted with them. They had unlimited sex and drank and ate their bodies into ruin. Paul explained to them

How does Jesus' death and resurrection affect your life today?

Jesus calls us to carry our own cross. What does that mean for you?

that this was against what God had said from the beginning—that creation was good. So we take care of our bodies in obedience to God and because we know that God can redeem our bodies and make them new.

Our confidence in the resurrection also helps us to take risks in following Christ. Paul connects the resurrection in a logical way to his own life as a traveling missionary. Paul could face the possibility of death every day because he knew that if he died, he could look forward to resurrection life with Christ. The resurrection helped give him courage to face the dangers that he had to face as a believer (1 Cor 15:30-34; Phil 1:21-26). The resurrection can also be a source of great strength for us today when we think about the risks and dangers of following Christ faithfully.

Summing it up:

- **The life, death, and resurrection of Jesus are at the heart of our faith.** Jesus died for our sins (1 Cor 15:3), opening a way for us to receive God's forgiveness and reconciliation. Jesus' death also shows us the power of faith and of God's love in the face of violence and evil. This has an impact on how we live as Jesus' followers.

- **Jesus showed that, by the way he lived his life, he was a threat to the powers that be.** When we follow Jesus, we too may face opposition from the world. But like Jesus, we look beyond suffering, even death, to our resurrection.

- **Jesus taught and modeled servant leadership.** True leaders, said Jesus, are those who serve. Jesus washed the disciples' feet. He demonstrated a power that is greater than any force on earth: the power of love.

- **Jesus was consistent to the end.** Especially at the time of his crucifixion, Jesus resisted the temptations he had faced in the wilderness. He refused to use force. He loved his enemies. He was obedient to God to the end. Ironically, when Jesus looked the weakest, hanging on the cross, he was the strongest. Satan, evil, and death were truly defeated through his obedience to God. The resurrection confirmed that victory.

- **The resurrection proved God's grace and love.** How can humans use their free will to sin horribly and yet see God make all things still work out? God stepped into that awesome tension by coming to our world in Jesus. God turned the very worst thing we could do—crucify Jesus—into the thing that defeated evil. We humans can do our worst—murder God—but we cannot destroy God's love for us.

a **spiritual discipline** to practice:

Get together with other Christians and have a footwashing service. Prepare some basins of warm water and have towels and chairs ready. Read John 13:1-17 and then, in twos, wash each other's feet. It may feel safer to wash feet with someone of your own gender. Then end the time with a hug. If you don't feel comfortable washing each other's feet, consider washing each other's hands instead.

Topics in chapter 6

- **The church is born**
- **One God, three persons**
- **God's new people: all people invited**
- **Conversion**
- **God's intervention in our lives**

Story line:
Jesus returns to heaven
The day of Pentecost
The early church
Peter and Cornelius
Paul's conversion

6. God's Spirit Moving

So. It looks like, feels like, it's all said and done. Jesus lived, died, and rose again. In some ways the problem seems solved. But if the Story stops here, we leave the disciples acting like scared chickens, cowering behind closed doors or fishing along lonely shores. They seem too afraid, too confused, to do anything. Is this what the new people of God are supposed to look like? The solution doesn't look like a good solution after all.

But wait. There's more to the Story. Just before Jesus returns to heaven following his resurrection, the disciples ask him: "Is this the time when you will restore the kingdom to Israel?" Jesus responds by getting them to look beyond their own nation. "It is not for you to know the times," he said. "You will receive power when the Holy Spirit has come upon you; and you will be my witnesses in Jerusalem, in all Judea and Samaria, and to the ends of the earth" (Acts 1:7-8). Jesus tells the disciples to wait. Even though Jesus has died and come back to life, other things need to happen. The disciples need something more.

Wind, flames, and speeches

So they waited. On the Jewish festival of Pentecost, they were all together to pray, as many as 120 of them. They were waiting—waiting

Something supernatural happens when we say yes to Jesus. Jesus comes to live inside us and we are changed. Isn't that what we talked about earlier—a change of identity? Well, isn't that the Holy Spirit? —*Rosella*

Trinity:

the classic belief among Christians that God exists in three "persons": Father (Creator), Son (Jesus, the Redeemer), and Holy Spirit (Sustainer)

God is One, but we experience God in different ways. So Christians have long believed in the Trinity, or the understanding that God the Creator, Jesus, and the Holy Spirit are the same God in three "persons" (see Matt 28:19-20; Acts 1:4-5; Rom 5:5-6; 2 Cor 13:13). That is, they share the same nature or essence. The Spirit and Jesus were both involved in creation (Ps 104:30; John 1:3). Just as Jesus is God incarnated in human form (see page 67–68), so also the Spirit is God's presence among us.

See the Confession of Faith summary of Article 1 about God on page 173.

for what, they didn't know. Suddenly, there comes this sound like a tornado, filling the house. Just as suddenly come little flames of fire, resting on each one of them. They look at each other. Can you imagine the fear? Then they begin to speak in other languages, tongues they don't know, speaking to everyone who will listen about the wonders of God. The Holy Spirit has come (Acts 2).

In one sense, these Jewish believers had no idea what was going on. In another sense, they did know. The strong wind reminded them of the wind over the Red Sea in the exodus (Exod 14:21). The fire on their heads recalled the pillar of fire (Exod 13:21). The different languages reminded them of the Tower of Babel (Gen 11:1-9). Only this time, everything was reversed. Instead of bringing confusion and separation, the Holy Spirit brought clarity and understanding. Foreign Jews visiting Jerusalem for the Pentecost festival heard words in their native tongues.

What did it mean? What phenomenon was so great that it reversed the effects of the Tower of Babel and came with all the symbols of the exodus? The Holy Spirit has come upon them. With this rush of mighty wind, there is a new being, an unexplainable presence among them, inside of them. It is the presence of Jesus.

Everything is different. Men and women who once cowered behind closed doors now preach in loud voices on the street corners (Acts 3:11-26). The ones who scattered after the crucifixion now live together as community, sharing food and possessions (Acts 2:43-47). With boldness, they heal the sick (Acts 3:1-10), preach repentance (Acts 2:38), and care for each other in radical ways (Acts 2:44-45; 6:1-7). They find themselves carrying on the work of Jesus in their own lives, in the strength of his Spirit.

The Holy Spirit's work was only beginning. Even though Jesus, through his life and death, defeated evil and made possible the solution to the sin problem, that solution had not quite reached its full potential.[1] As the early disciples saw things, God's salvation was designed mainly for the Jews. It would take another series of events before they would remember how God called Abraham so that all peoples could be blessed (Gen 12:3). It would take some special events for them to remember even Jesus' own teaching that God loved non-Jews as well as Jews. In a nutshell, the whole book of Acts is that story of how God's ultimate plan begins to unfold: the creation of a people from all ethnic groups and backgrounds (Luke 3:4-6; Rev 5:9-10).

See the Confession of Faith summary of Article 3 about the Holy Spirit and Article 18 about Christian spirituality (pages 173, 176).

Who is the Holy Spirit?

Mary: Thinking about the Spirit is weird for me. Exactly who is the Holy Spirit?

Rosella: The Spirit of Jesus who came to us after Jesus ascended (Rom 8:9).

Josh: Well, not an impersonal force—not a "May-the-force- be-with-you" kind of thing.

Tara: The Spirit is our Advocate (John 14:16).

Josh: Our Agitator, too (John 16:8).

Michele: The Holy Spirit offers gifts—abilities to do God's work and for building up the church (1 Cor 12–14).

Rosella: Don't forget the fruit of the Spirit: love, joy, peace, patience, kindness, generosity, faithfulness, gentleness, and self-control (Gal 5:22-23). I think these are more important than the gifts of the Spirit (see 1 Cor 12:8-11; also Eph 4:11-13); if gifts aren't accompanied by love, they're worthless.

Luke: The Holy Spirit brings unity. If there is fighting and division, then people are not letting the Holy Spirit really work (1 Cor 2:6–3:4).

Mike: That doesn't mean conflict is bad.

Luke: Exactly. But the real proof that you have the Spirit is whether or not you love each other enough to work through the conflict (Eph 4:3).

Tara: You should not stifle the Holy Spirit. I think that if the Spirit tells you to do something, you better do it. But—oh boy, here comes a confession—if you watch TV all the time, it's probably hard to hear the Spirit telling you to do anything (Isa 63:10; Eph 4:30; 1 Thess 5:19).

Rosella: The Holy Spirit is an advocate for us (Rom 8:26-27). When my soul is heavy with worry, with grief, I just know that the Spirit is praying with me and for me in ways that I can't even understand.

A whole new way of seeing things. It started in a rather small way. One day, God asks Peter, through a bizarre vision, to eat animals that good Jews considered unclean to eat (Acts 10). Peter is stunned. This vision is asking him to go against everything he believes is right and good. He is already stretching it by staying at Simon's house, a man himself unclean because of his occupation as a tanner. But this? To *eat* unclean animals was to disobey God.

At the same time, in a town not far away, a Roman centurion named Cornelius also received a vision. In it, God instructs him to send for Peter. But what a dilemma! Peter, as a good Jew, would never enter the house of a Gentile like Cornelius. Nevertheless, Cornelius sends his servants on this strange mission.

When the Spirit nudges

While I was working on a new book, I was struggling, not knowing what to say, wondering if God could even use me to write. Then I suddenly heard a voice.

It was 10:30 at night and the office building was locked. Nobody could get in. But it was my friend Neil. He had this strange look on his face. He said, "Don't laugh, but I think God sent me here." He was walking home, saw my light on, and felt God telling him to go see me. He said to God, "If the door is open, I'll know you want me to go see Michele."

The most amazing thing was that the door should have been locked, and yet he walked right in. We checked the door and sure enough, it was locked from the outside. There was no way he should have been able to get in. Now I believe firmly that the Holy Spirit spoke to Neil that night, instructing him to encourage me, even though Neil didn't even know what I was doing. Nothing really spectacular happened as we talked, but I just felt this presence, this love of God pouring over me. God cared enough about me to send a friend at the right time.

That's what makes Christianity so exciting. I think God wants to whisper in our ears and have this intimate conversation with us, where God actually tells us, "Go see this person" or "Send a note of encouragement to so and so." —*Michele*

Meanwhile, the unclean animals keep descending in Peter's vision. A second and third time, a voice from heaven says, "What God has made clean, you must not call profane." Then, with perfect timing, just as the servants from Cornelius approach the house, the Spirit speaks to Peter, telling him to go with them without hesitation. All these miraculous things combine to help Peter experience a new conversion, a conversion to a brand-new understanding about God. "I truly understand that God shows no partiality," he says when he meets Cornelius (Acts 10:34-35). And while he speaks, the Holy Spirit descends on Cornelius and all who were hearing the gospel there. This was proof beyond a shadow of a doubt. All people could become a part of the people of God.

Peter's Vision —Guercino

What kind of a church will we have? Word of Cornelius's conversion reached the other Christians—100 percent of whom were Jewish, remember—and many did not know what to make of the whole thing. It became an even bigger question as Paul and Barnabas, sent by believers in Antioch, began to travel to other regions and attracted more non-Jews to the Christian faith. The big question for the church now was: How would Gentiles become part of the church? Did the men need to be circumcised, as men among God's people always had been, ever since Abraham? Put another way, did people need to become Jews first before they could be true Christians? Some Jewish Christians were actively teaching that they did, but Peter's experience with the vision seemed to indicate otherwise. Paul and Barnabas, who had seen many Gentiles turn to Christ, also argued vigorously that it shouldn't matter.

As Acts 15 tells it, the leaders of the church finally get together in Jerusalem to discuss this new situation. There is a lot at stake. Would there be two kinds of Christians—Jewish Christians (first rate) and Gentile Christians (second rate)? What do Gentiles need to do to become part of the church? Are ethnicity and religious rituals (like circumcision) important for salvation, now that the church proclaims that Jesus is Lord of all people? What will this new people of God look like?

The big decision. The believers at the Jerusalem conference prayed. They went over the facts. They tried to discern the truth together. And they decided in the end that there would only be one church and that anyone could be a Christian without becoming a Jew first. The Gentile male believers did not have to be circumcised (undoubtedly to their relief!). From that moment on, Paul, Barnabas, Timothy, and others were sent on new mission trips with new freedom to welcome Gentiles around the world into God's new community. (The problem of "Judaizers," however, didn't go away. Paul's letters often argue against those who wanted to insist on circumcision or to make Gentile Christians second class.)

Peter Teaches Cornelius —H. Miller

What an incredible feat! God's original plan, God's original desire starting with Abraham and Sarah, was now fulfilled. People who normally hated each other were eating at the same table, praying together, staying in each other's homes. The new people of God came from every tribe and nation, and all of them were equal in God's eyes. That's what Paul meant when he wrote about no "Jew or Gentile, slave or free, male or female" in the church (Gal 3:28). That doesn't mean that ethnic, social, and gender distinctions disappeared. But they no longer formed boundaries of who's better, or who's in and who's out.

Living it out

Huns and Barbarians: One Sunday morning in 1996, a few Korean families showed up at Charleswood Mennonite Church in Winnipeg. They were a long way from home. They came because they had heard about the 16th-century Anabaptists and wanted to study at Canadian Mennonite Bible College; and they also wanted to become a part of a Mennonite church. They were intrigued with the peace teachings of Jesus and the emphasis on making decisions as a covenant community. They were used to living life in a much more hierarchical and militaristic way, and they longed for something different. Through promptings of the Spirit, they showed up at our church one day.

A relationship began to develop. They asked many questions, and sometimes we were uncomfortable when they saw us in such a good light. What if they would be disappointed? We are not perfect—far from it. And yet the Spirit of God was prompting us, too, to enter into a relationship. Over the next years, I was struck by the fact that those of us from European background are descended from Barbarians. Those from Korean background are descended from Huns. More than 1,500 years ago Huns and Barbarians were killing each other. Now the Holy Spirit had brought us together to put peace into practice and to make decisions as one community under the leadership of Jesus. I think of this as one of the surprises of the Spirit—that Huns and Barbarians could follow the Prince of Peace together.

—*John Braun, Winnipeg, Manitoba*

New creation. God wanted to—and did—create not only a beautiful physical world, but a people as well. God dreamed of a people whose identity was not in their family line but in their saying yes to God—a community built on trust and obedience. This is what Paul writes about in 2 Corinthians 5:17: "So if anyone is in Christ, there is a new creation: everything old has passed away; see, everything has become new!"

Some people see this new creation as only an individual, personal conversion. It's true that when we begin to follow Jesus and accept

Think of some examples in which people you know have been changed positively through their encounter with God.

See the Confession of Faith summaries of Articles 9 and 16 about the church on page 174 and 176.

the grace he has to offer us, something new is created within us. But even more, Paul is talking about the church as the new creation. The "new creation" is about a radical new way of living here on earth, as God's new people. People who are normally enemies actually worship together (Eph 2:11-22). Race, gender, social status, and religious backgrounds don't matter any more. This radical way was incredibly good news in Paul's ethnically and socially divided society, and it continues to be so for us as well.

Salvation involves both the individual and the church. Nobody understood the importance of individual faith as well as the Anabaptists (see chapter 9). They understood that each person had to make his or her own decision to follow Jesus. At the same time, baptism made you a part of a community of people who supported each other, cared for each other, and had a common commitment to live the Jesus way together. They didn't believe that you could live the Christian life by yourself.

Josh: This is new info for me—that the new creation is really the church when it includes both Jews and Gentiles? What about accepting Jesus as your Savior?

Luke: I wouldn't totally debunk the whole you-and-Jesus thing. I just think it is even better news when it includes whole communities. Catholics and Protestants in Northern Ireland finally coming together—that's what is happening here. That's new creation.

Tara: That sounds more miraculous than the parting of the Red Sea.

Luke: Maybe it is.

The miracles continue

Because of the Holy Spirit, the church grew by leaps and bounds (Acts 2:41). Miracles continued (Acts 5:12-16). The believers voluntarily shared their possessions and money, some selling everything and putting the money in a common pot (Acts 4:32-37). They opened up their homes as places to host church gatherings and put up traveling preachers (Acts 16:15).

Have you joined the community of the Spirit, the church? If so, what signs of the Spirit do you see there?

Paul. One of the biggest proofs that God was doing extraordinary things was a man named Saul, later to be known as Paul. Saul was a strict Jew, a Pharisee, which meant he had a particular idea of what the Messiah would be like. He wasn't that different from us; we all see and understand God through the lens of our background and culture. Saul, however, felt God wanted him to oppose this new Jesus movement. Jesus couldn't be the Messiah, Saul felt, because the Bible said that anyone hung on a tree was cursed (Deut 21:23).

One day, while on his way to the city of Damascus to arrest more believers, a great light suddenly shone all around him. Blinded, he fell to his knees. "Saul, Saul, why do you persecute me?" said a voice from thin air. "I am Jesus, whom you are persecuting" (Acts 9:1-19). From that instant on, Saul knew that Jesus was the Christ. He knew that he had met the risen Lord. In the following days and years, more of the pieces fell into place as he learned the Jesus Story. But most importantly, Saul now followed Jesus as passionately as he had opposed him before. Saul now became known as Paul—the greatest promoter of Jesus in the first century.

Paul's Conversion —A. Eitzen

Conversion

Luke: I always felt guilty about the way I became a Christian. I was 11 or 12 at church camp and we were sitting around the campfire. The speaker started playing on my emotions just a little bit. As he closed, we all sang four verses of "It Only Takes a Spark." I was sitting next to Vicky, and I just couldn't wait till "Walk a Mile" (a handholding game), because—you know the hormonal tension of adolescence.

So I was really concentrating on Vicky. Meanwhile, in the last five minutes the speaker got really serious, and Vicky was really keyed in to him. Then he asked people who wanted to make a commitment to Jesus to come forward. Vicky went forward—so I went forward, too. I wondered, Did I just go forward because she did? Did I get something out of that?

I prayed a "repeat-after-me" prayer to invite Christ into my life. Not long after, I went through the faith exploration class and got baptized, and the church celebrated. And this whole time, I wasn't sure if this one counted or not. Eventually, though, my faith came along and I got real with God. But it was a disastrous beginning.

Michele: That's the wonder of God. Despite the rough beginning, you do have a relationship with Jesus. God still worked in you. If we lose sight of it as a journey and think only about the moment of conversion, as if that's when the Christian faith is over and done, then we lose a lot.

Not every encounter with Jesus was so dramatic. Other people, like Nathaniel, came to follow Jesus after much thought (John 1:43-51). Some, like Peter, said yes impulsively, then struggled with that commitment (John 21:15-19). Today, too, the Holy Spirit works with each of us in unique ways. Some experience dramatic conversions. Some feel like they've always loved and followed Jesus, as much as they know how. Some weigh the pros and cons, or the proofs, more than others do. All, though, can take a beginning step of faith in what will become the most beautiful, thrilling journey there is.

The choice is ours. After we begin this awesome journey of faith, the ride is never predictable. Sometimes we just know the Spirit is speaking to us and at other times we wonder if it's just indigestion. Some Christians know immediately what their mission in life or their spiritual gift is, while others wait patiently and wonder. The hardest times can be when you don't particularly feel the Spirit at all. Does that mean the Spirit isn't there anymore? No. It just means that Christianity is more than our feelings and that the Holy Spirit moves freely.

We can't program God the way the Canaanites tried to program their Baal gods (see page 59). The Holy Spirit is anything but predictable, except for this one thing: the Spirit of Jesus is here to help us, guide us, and love us (Rom 14:17; Gal 5:22; 1 Thess 1:6; Acts 9:31; John 15:26; Rom 5:3-5; Rom 15:13; Gal 5:5; John 14:16-17). The Spirit intends to change the world through us. The Spirit wants to do wonderful things through us, just like the Spirit did through the people in the Bible. On the other hand, the Spirit will never force us. The choice rests with us to be open and ready to move when the Spirit moves.

Note: Chapter 8 talks in more detail about the gifts of the Spirit—abilities that God gives us to be God's instruments of blessing in the church and in the world.

How have you noticed the Spirit calling you—either to begin a relationship with Jesus, or to deepen your trust and obedience? When have you wondered whether certain events or "nudgings" in your life are the work of God's Spirit?

You may also feel discouraged when you see Christians—including yourself—fail to live up to their claims. How does that affect your confidence in the Holy Spirit?

Summing it up:

- **Jesus lives on in us, the church, through the Holy Spirit.** As the early believers waited and prayed, the Spirit of Christ came and changed them into people who would take the good news—the Story—to the world. The Holy Spirit can work like that in us, too.

- **God, Jesus, and the Holy Spirit are one.** The Christian belief in the Trinity helps us see how the presence and work of the Spirit in our lives today is really the continuing presence and work of Jesus. In Jesus, God has shown God's own self in our world. As we say yes to Jesus, the Spirit moves into our lives and transforms us.

- **The Spirit works through the church.** The story of the church's beginning is really the story of the Holy Spirit. Christians don't live in isolation as individuals. The surest sign that we have the Spirit is the unity we experience with Christian sisters and brothers. The church is constantly growing and developing as God's "new creation." But the Spirit works in each of us to build up the church and to build our character toward what God intends for us.

- **When the Spirit is present, human divisions break down.** The early church had to make a 180-degree change in their thinking as they realized that Jesus had broken every barrier to God, including ethnic barriers. Christian unity is a sign of the Spirit's work today, too.

[1] Inspired by scholarly lectures by Marion Bontrager, Hesston College, Hesston, Kansas.

a **spiritual discipline** to practice:

Get together with other Christians and brainstorm about the barriers that the church community might unintentionally be putting up. Then spend time in prayer and ask the Holy Spirit to speak to you, giving you discernment. As you pray, listen for the Spirit to give you a task to do or perhaps a new person to call—some new opportunity for you to welcome others.

Topics in chapter 7

- **God meets us where we are**
- **Salvation—another look**
- **Saying yes to the Story (steps to becoming a Christian)**
- **Baptism**
- **Joining God's people, the church**
- **The Lord's Supper—communion**

Story line:
Our own lives
Apostle Paul's letters

7. God's Story, My Story, Our Story

In the last six chapters we have pondered the Story—the story of God in the world. The climax of that Story was and is Jesus. And like all who have met him in person, we must decide for ourselves how to respond to Jesus. "Who do you say I am?" Jesus asked Peter—and he asks the same of us. Jesus longs for us, like Peter, to say that he is the Messiah, the Son of the living God. He longs for us to leave our fishing nets and follow him.

Scratching where it itches. In the New Testament, Jesus uses many ways of helping people find what they most need. Some people have their physical or social needs met as they come to Jesus (the widow in Luke 7:11-17). Some people have their whole worldview turned upside down when they meet him (Nathaniel in John 1:43-51 or Paul in Acts 9:1-22). Often, Jesus declares forgiveness to those who feel an overwhelming burden of sin (Peter in Luke 5:1-11). For the woman caught in adultery, Jesus says, "Neither do I condemn you. Go your way, and from now on do not sin again" (John 8:1-11), giving her grace and calling her to holiness all at the same time.

I'm tempted to make it very simple—and in some ways it is very simple. I want to emphasize a relationship with Jesus. Getting up every morning, knowing I'm God's child. The Master of the whole universe wants to talk to me, change the world through me. —*Rosella*

A rich young leader who had done everything right in his life still felt a spiritual restlessness. To him, Jesus says, "Go and sell your possessions" (Luke 18:18-30). But in the very next story about another rich man, Zacchaeus, Jesus doesn't say, "Zach, give up your cheating ways." Instead, he says, "I must stay at your house today" (Luke 19:1-10). Out of that experience of hospitality, Zacchaeus's life is transformed. Somehow Jesus knew what each person needed to hear. He knew that Zacchaeus needed to hear grace, while the only hope for the young leader lay in the hard call to leave his wealth.

It's that way for us, too. Jesus knows exactly what we need and offers us salvation in the way that fits our need. Some of us, if we're honest, need a good jolt. We're prideful and full of ourselves. So the words of Jesus might sound abrasive to us, but yet, down deep, we know they ring true. Others of us are so filled with shame for things we've done that we can't even look Jesus in the eye. For us, Jesus offers such love and gentleness that we can find freedom and forgiveness and, in that, find the power to leave our sin behind.

You may not have heard about salvation in ways that are helpful to you. Unlike Jesus, fellow Christians can't know completely what you need. But that's one reason why there are so many different pictures of salvation in the Bible—they speak to our needs as humans, in all our complexity.

> **holiness:**
>
> 1) a way of expressing the total otherness and purity of God. Part of becoming holy means refraining from sin and imitating God's own character. 2) being set apart or called out for a special job (Lev 20:26)

Zacchaeus —A. Eitzen

So what can we say with assurance about salvation?

For all the different pictures given to us in the Bible, there are some common threads that run through them.

grace:
kindness and mercy, which we can do nothing to earn

It's "a relationship thing." Remember the stories from Genesis that help define the problem of sin (page 22–25)? Salvation mends and heals all the relationships that sin breaks—our relationships with God, others, ourselves, and all of creation. This makes salvation so much more than just believing in Jesus. Yes, we do believe in Jesus, but it's the kind of "believing" that affects and changes our whole life—including our relationships.

If salvation means following Jesus in a relationship, then that means it is ongoing. When we first say yes to Jesus as Savior and Lord, it is a beginning, not an end. Some people think that as soon as they see their children or friends get baptized they can wipe their brows

---

Faith as a journey

Luke: I think salvation is a journey. I renew my relationship with God; I work at it more diligently some times than other times, but it's a journey. I don't like the idea I heard when I was younger that salvation was this one-time experience. No one really talked to me about what happened after my "conversion."

Josh: What did happen?

Luke: I didn't have it all together. There were still things I had to learn. I was still tempted. You name it.

Michele: It is a journey. At the same time, most people need a definite starting point, even if they have always known God, always loved Jesus. Depending on personalities and background, some people need a big conversion experience while some need a gradual coming to commitment. Some people can point to a definite moment when they said yes to Jesus. Others can't pinpoint the date but they know they've made a decision. Baptism is an important way they tell the world that they've started the journey.

and say, "Whoosh, I'm glad they did that," as if the baptism closed the deal and now they don't have to worry about their loved ones anymore. Like every other relationship, it's a journey.

It's a "God thing." Salvation comes to us through God. In the Story, God makes the first move—always. "While we still were sinners Christ died for us," writes Paul (Rom 5:8). We can have a relationship with God and be transformed because of the faithfulness of Jesus, not because we have such wonderful faith ourselves.

The Holy Spirit comes to each of us and—in different ways for different people—nudges us toward God. We can say no to the Holy Spirit; God does not coerce us into following Christ. But we take on faith that the Holy Spirit whispers to us what we need to hear, even if the message may be hard to hear (Luke 18:18-30).

When we do say yes, a supernatural, unexplainable, incredibly wonderful thing happens to us. This is the part of salvation that is hardest to understand. God changes us. God makes us into new people. The Holy Spirit lives inside of us and we find ourselves "in Christ." God forgives our sins and begins to break the bondage of sin so that we are free to become what we were created to be. We have a new identity. We are transformed (Rom 6:1-14).

> **Salvation** *is* a matter of life and death. But that's different than believing it's a matter of life *after* death.

This happens whether we feel it or not. Christianity is more than a set of feelings. It's more than some emotional high that we sometimes get at camp or a big worship event—wonderful as that is. Since our experience with God is a journey, it will have ups and downs. And when our experience with Jesus looks different from the experiences of other Christians, it doesn't mean their experiences are real and ours are not. God is God, and not some cosmic pop machine. God works differently with different people as God sees fit.

It's an "us thing." As much as it is a God thing, it is also an us thing. Jesus never forced anyone to follow him, and that holds for us as well. The Holy Spirit invites us to follow Christ and join God's people, and we must decide whether or not to accept the invitation. That is true even if we come from families who have been Christians for many generations. Each one of us has the privilege and the responsibility to say yes or no. It's true that if we're not careful, we can put so much emphasis on our part and our response that salvation becomes little more than good works that we use like a merit badge to get us into heaven. Salvation is still about God and God's work in and for us. But it is about us in the sense that we have to accept this wonderful gift that God offers us. We must dare to believe that Jesus loves us this much, that the Creator of this world, out of love, wants to have a friendship with us, wants to care for us.

It's a "repentance thing." The bare-bones message that Jesus and his followers proclaimed was, "The kingdom of God has come near; repent, and believe in the good news" (Mark 1:15). Meeting Jesus means you eventually also come face-to-face with your own worst enemy—the sin in your life. Like Peter when he first met Jesus, we come to the point of praying, "Go away from me, Lord, for I am a sinful man" (Luke 5:8). (Of course, Jesus didn't leave him; Jesus called Peter to follow him.)

repent:
to turn from sin and commit oneself to a change of life

Repentance, as it is understood in the Bible, means a lot more than saying "I'm sorry." Repentance means turning our life around 180 degrees. It means orienting our behavior so that we now follow God's way, not our own. Such a turnaround is impossible on our own strength. But that's where the Holy Spirit works in us in supernatural ways, right from when we say yes to Jesus. Would the Story truly be "good news" if we had to remain in our sin for the rest of our lives? Would it truly be "good news" if we didn't ask and receive forgiveness from each other and by God's help mend those relationships? No, our salvation starts right now, and that is really good news.

As we confront and confess our sin, God forgives both the bad things we have done and the good things we have failed to do (1 John 1:9). But God doesn't just leave us there. The Holy Spirit gives us what we need to live lives that are radically different from the rest of the world. When everyone else looks after number one, we put the interests of others first (Phil 2:4). When others dominate, we serve each other by washing each other's feet (John 13). When the rest of the world loves only those who love them back, we go beyond that and love our enemy (Matt 5:43-48), not because we have to, but because that is who we are. That is how children of God act—just like their heavenly Parent.

It means Jesus is Savior and Lord of our lives. Sometimes we talk about Jesus as our Savior, and at other times we speak of Jesus as Lord. Both of these realities are important, and they work together in us. We must remember that there is nothing, *nothing*, we can do to earn God's favor. We all mess up. We are all in need of the gracious gift of salvation that God offers us through Jesus. We can't save ourselves. Only Jesus can.

But Jesus must also be the Lord of our lives. Something or someone is lord when they have our first and total allegiance. Whatever is first priority is lord. At the time of the early church, people throughout the Roman Empire were required to declare "Caesar is Lord." If they refused to do this in a public setting, they could be arrested and punished. But for Christian believers, this was a dilemma. Jesus and Caesar could not both be Lord. Christians had to choose—sometimes at the risk of their own lives. Who would give them the most security? To whom would their loyalties go? What was the most "real" reality?

Saying "Jesus is Lord" might not get us killed in Canada or the United States, but the choice is still the same. Jesus and government cannot get equal loyalty from us. We cannot put our ultimate security in both Jesus and the force of arms. To put anything else ahead of Jesus is to make an idol of it, to make it lord instead of Jesus. If and when the laws of our land contradict God's laws, we obey God first (Acts 5:29).

It goes even deeper than that. The world can win over our loyalty in very subtle ways. If Jesus is really Lord of our lives, then all the social barriers that the world says are a big deal—race, gender, economics, being "cool" in school—are not a big deal to us. Because Jesus was Lord in the early church (and ethnicity was not), Jews ate with Gentiles and slaves worshiped with their masters. This was unheard of elsewhere in the world. It was a miracle as great as the crossing of the Red Sea.

What things are we tempted to serve as our lord instead of Jesus? For some people, it's always needing the latest clothes, or the pressure to be popular, or putting our trust in the military. Read and discuss the Confession of Faith summary of Article 23 about where we place our trust.

Living it out

For a long time, the "need to be right" kept me from surrendering all of my life to God. I searched and argued long and hard for all the "right" answers to any question, issue, or problem I faced. And I sometimes wouldn't stop debating until the other person saw that I was "right." It is a positive thing to be analytical and stand up for what you believe in. However, "needing to be right" prevented me from seeing things from another perspective and allowed me to be judgmental. My need to be right came from a fear of imperfection and "doing the wrong thing" in a certain situation or in my life's direction. Through my work at an organization dedicated to nonviolence, I am invited every day to relinquish the "need to be right" and, instead, to simply be faithful, as best as I know how at that moment, to God who is full of steadfast love and wisdom. God knows all and holds all, and it is okay if I can't see the whole picture before taking action. A Christian ethic of nonviolence means I am open to the constant process of confession, change, and affirmation. —*Sarah Thompson, Elkhart, Indiana*

Salvation means being with God forever. What awesome news! We have a home in heaven when we die. We can be with Jesus forever. Salvation is not just for here on earth. We will live after we die. We will experience resurrection. Every tear that has fallen will be dried. When times are tough, we can feel comfort in knowing this. A day will come when we will see Jesus! (John 14:1-7; Rev 21:1-4; Phil 1:21-26).

So what do I do? Saying yes to Jesus

Till now, we have been describing salvation—the Story of God as it touches the world and as it touches our lives. In that description we've referred to some of the responses that this Story calls out in us. If you're wondering what it takes to clinch that decision to follow Jesus, here is a summary:

1. Choose God's Story as your own. Out of all the ways of understanding who we are and why we are, we choose the Story of how God has been loving and drawing us through Jesus Christ. Salvation is a love story, a love story where the Creator of the universe reaches out in incredible ways—even from the cross—to help us see that we are loved and to help us accept and trust this love. As we begin this trust, this relationship, the Story defines our identity and our way of looking at the world. We "believe" in Jesus.

2. Receive God's forgiveness and grace. We all need to be reconciled with God. God, through Jesus, provides what we need to be forgiven and restored to a relationship with God. We experience that forgiveness as we repent—confessing our sin and asking God to empower us to live faithfully.

3. Join God's people. All along, God has been creating a people who follow in God's way. Salvation is not just an individual experience. It involves being part of God's people and joining in God's mission to the world.

4. Follow Jesus with joyful gratitude. We follow Jesus as Savior and Lord—not because we have to—but because we don't have to. In the strength of the Holy Spirit, we not only can follow Jesus, but we want to do it. We live in joyful gratitude for all God has done for us. It's the hardest thing and yet the most joyous thing—all at the same time.[2]

What is your experience of salvation? Have you had a dramatic encounter with God? Or have you come to faith more gradually?

Jesus Calling Fishermen —A. Bida

Baptism and Anabaptism

The step of baptism has always been important for Anabaptists, the part of the Christian church that includes Mennonites. *Anabaptist* is a fancy word for "rebaptizer." In the 1500s in Europe, Anabaptists rejected the state church's practice of baptizing all infants in the society. For Anabaptists, baptism signified a personal decision to follow Christ, a decision that would be impossible for a baby to make. They looked at the Bible and could find no examples of infant baptism. What they did find were people receiving baptism as evidence of their commitment to Jesus.

The Anabaptists, therefore, rebaptized believing adults who had already been baptized as infants, and they refused to have their own babies baptized. This civil disobedience was a threat to the state church. It defied the state's authority, but, even more importantly, it messed up the system of counting people for taxation. Infant baptism was part of the process of becoming a citizen.

By not baptizing their babies, Anabaptists were also making the statement that church and state should not be one and the same. A citizen of Germany, for example, should not automatically be considered a Christian. If that were the case, then the best way to spread Christianity would be to conquer other governments by force and make people Christians by making them citizens of the state. (This actually was how Christianity often did spread from the fourth century on, when Christianity became the official religion of the Roman Empire. Later, during the Crusades, "Christian" soldiers made their captives become Christians at the point of a sword.)

Chapter 9 has more about the Anabaptists. Also, see the Confession of Faith summary of Article 11 on page 175 about baptism.

Baptism: Going Public

Saying yes to Jesus may feel like an overwhelming step, but it is a wonderful, life-changing step, too. Christians make that decision public through the church's ritual of baptism with water. People have a lot of questions about baptism. Is it just a ritual? Does it have some power to bring us salvation? Do we have to be baptized in order to be a Christian or to go to heaven? Is it something you are supposed to do at a certain age because that's the tradition in our church?

Here are a few things that the Bible says about baptism:

Baptism is a sign of faith. On the day of Pentecost, those who welcomed Peter's message about Jesus were baptized and added to the company of Jesus' followers (Acts 2:41-42). Baptism in the New Testament is always associated with repentance and faith.

Baptism is an aid to faith. Baptism symbolizes and reminds us of our new life in Christ (Rom 6:1-4; see the significance of the modes of baptism below). Like other rituals, it has no special power in itself and it doesn't guarantee a miracle or a spiritual high. But neither is it an empty practice without meaning. Like other rituals, it helps open us up to experience God in a new way.

Baptism shows obedience to God's call. Jesus himself was launched into his mission in life at the time of his baptism. In baptism we show our readiness to participate in carrying God's Story forward (Matt 3:13-17). Jesus instructed his disciples to go and make disciples throughout the world, baptizing and teaching them to observe his teachings (Matt 28:19-20).

Baptism is a pledge. Baptism shows publicly that we are prepared to be part of the "body of Christ," the church (Gal 3:26-28). This new life with God will be lived out in the context of a local congregation. It is a commitment to faith, accountability, and ministry (Rom 6:1-11).

Baptism is *not* a rite of passage. Being baptized at a standard age or grade in school isn't much better than getting baptized as a baby. It needs to happen after we have made our own commitment to Jesus. That happens at different ages for different people.

Baptism is *not* recognition of achievement. Baptism isn't a sign that we have passed a faith exploration class or that we are now spiritually mature. Baptism is a sign of what God has done for us in Christ, not what we have achieved for God.

Different styles, different pictures of God's work

Sprinkling, pouring, and immersion are three forms of baptism that the church has used over the ages. Each way has biblical foundations, and each one emphasizes a special aspect of salvation.

Sprinkling reminds us of the Jewish sacrificial system. The priests would sprinkle the blood of an animal against the sides of the altar (Lev 7:2; 16:14). Christians took this ancient ritual and applied it to Jesus in Hebrews 10:22: "Let us approach with a true heart in full assurance of faith, with our hearts sprinkled clean from an evil conscience and our bodies washed with pure water." When the baptismal water is sprinkled over new believers, it pictures their cleansing from sin and guilt through the death of Jesus.

Pouring recalls the anointing of Jewish high priests as they were consecrated for service (Exod 29:7). In the New Testament, God "poured out" the Holy Spirit (Acts 2:17, 33; 10:45; Titus 3:6). When water is poured upon baptismal candidates, it pictures the coming of the Holy Spirit in their lives and their complete dedication to serving Jesus.

Immersion symbolizes death and resurrection. Candidates are "dunked" in a tank, a lake, or some other body of water. The Israelites came through the Red Sea, leaving behind their old lives of slavery and rising to their new freedom as God's people. The apostle Paul talks about believers burying their old, sinful lives in baptism and rising to new life in Christ (Rom 6:1-4; 1 Cor 10:1-2; Col 2:12). Peter connects baptism with Noah's flood, which "buried" a sinful world (1 Pet 3:19-21). And so today, immersion can be a symbol of our death to sin and our rising to new life through Jesus.

J. Patinir

El Greco

Giotto

Baptism and the Holy Spirit. The New Testament speaks of Christians being baptized by one Spirit (1 Cor 12:13). Water baptism and the coming of the Holy Spirit are closely connected, even though the Bible doesn't show a particular sequence of events. When Jesus is baptized, the Holy Spirit rests on Jesus right at the time of his baptism (John 1:33). In the book of Acts, some people receive a "baptism" of special signs of the Holy Spirit before they are baptized by water (Acts 10:44-48). Others receive water baptism first (Acts 8:14-16). The Holy Spirit comes to us in unique ways as we say yes to Jesus. The Spirit gives us special gifts for ministry as we do God's work (Eph 4:1-16; 1 Cor 12). The Spirit also produces the "fruit" of love, joy, peace, patience, kindness, generosity, faithfulness, gentleness, and self-control (Gal 5:22).

Church membership

Michele: What do you think about membership?

Tara: It's good. It's important.

Michele: Should it be associated with baptism?

Mike: We've talked all along about how being a Christian is becoming a part of the people of God. So, yes, this makes sense.

Michele: But some people want to get baptized but not become a member. Why wouldn't they want to become a member?

Tara: Oh, now I see where you're coming from. Well, if the church is mediocre, then I wouldn't want to join. If Christians don't do what they say, who would want that?

Mike: You can be a Christian without being a member of a specific church—technically. You shouldn't confuse the two. But you have to be a part of the people of God—some local church—somewhere.

Tara: Instead of churches going nuts about people not wanting to join, they need to look at why they don't want to and get some—some life pumped into them.

Joining a family of faith: church membership

For Mennonites and many other Christians, baptism is connected with becoming a member of a local congregation. We cannot live our Christian lives as islands to ourselves. Saying yes to Jesus makes us part of a spiritual family of followers. That family is always a group of real people, not some symbolic association. God is still creating a people, not a bunch of individuals with their tickets to heaven. We need each other for support, accountability, and help in discernment. The apostle Paul talks to the Corinthians about being God's "temple" (1 Cor 3:16-17) and the "body of Christ." Both are pictures of something made up of many parts that depend on each other (see page 162).

The church is not a club. Membership in a church is different from membership in a club. In today's society, we are flooded with offers to be a member of some club. "Membership has its privileges," one credit card company says. Becoming a member of most organizations is a breeze. You pay the dues or you do some special little thing, and you're in. Most people join because it benefits them. Many want their clubs to keep "undesirable" people out.

Membership in the church is not like that at all. No one can be kept from being part of God's people because of race or gender or income. Membership is free. At the same time, the standards of the church are higher than any other group. It costs you everything—your life. That doesn't mean that you will die when you become a church member or that you will have to give up all your money—but it might, if that is what God calls you to do.

And we don't join a local congregation to get something, even though there are benefits to being a part of the church. We do it because that's who we are in Christ. We do it as part of our worship

See the Confession of Faith summary of Article 9 on page 174 about the church.

and obedience to God. Just think how different some worship experiences might be if people came with the desire to *give* something instead of expecting to *get* something.

Food and drink for the journey: the Lord's Supper

The church's odd combination of high standards (living Jesus' way) and open membership is as strange to the world as aliens from Mars. Yet, what holds it all together is love. This incredible love is celebrated and nurtured in what we call the Lord's Supper, or communion. In this ritual, Christians gather to remember and proclaim the death of Jesus.

As Jesus did with his disciples on the Thursday night before his crucifixion, we eat bread and drink grape juice (Luke 22:14-23). We remember the exodus, when God freed a group of slaves from Pharaoh's oppression. We especially celebrate the new reality that Jesus introduced. The broken bread is a sign of Christ's body, which

Christ Washes the Disciples' Feet
—D. van Baburen

was broken on the cross. The grape juice is a sign of Christ's blood shed for us. As we eat the bread and drink the cup, we recognize Jesus' presence, and we open our hearts in a fuller way to Jesus and to each other.

Jesus spoke of the bread and the cup as signs of the new covenant that God makes with us through his death (Matt 26:28; Mark 14:24; Luke 22:20; see page 47). Like the covenants in the Old Testament, this final covenant comes through God's initiative and God's love for the world. As often as we take communion, we reaffirm our own side of the agreement: we say again that we want to live Jesus' life.

The "each other" part of communion. We can say all the right words and respect the ritual of the bread and cup, but if we have a grudge against someone else in the church, we might as well not do communion at all (1 Cor 11:17-22, 27-34). We must take care to resolve conflicts among ourselves, confess our sins to each other, and ask and offer forgiveness. Only together can we be the body of Christ (1 Cor 12). Without love for each other, the ritual of communion is empty and we do not experience the Spirit of Jesus within us (1 Cor 13; 1 John 4:20).

Washing each other's feet. In many Mennonite communion services, this love for each other is expressed also through the footwashing ritual. Just like communion and baptism, footwashing cannot bring us salvation. It does not automatically produce love in us. It's not a requirement of being a Christian (in fact, many Mennonite groups do not have this tradition at all). Yet it can be a way of reinforcing our call to lay down our power and to serve others. God placed all things into Jesus' hands (John 13:3), and yet on the eve of his crucifixion, he laid it all aside as he demonstrated his love by washing the disciples' feet. He told them, and he tells us, to do the same (John 13:14).

See the Confession of Faith summaries for Articles 12 and 13 on page 175 about communion and footwashing.

Think about all the times in your life when you have watched or participated in baptism, communion, or footwashing. What have they meant to you?

Summing it up:

- **Salvation is both an event and a journey.** It is a transformation that God initiates in our lives and to which we must say yes. It is completely free, yet costs us everything. It changes us instantly, and yet we keep on being transformed for the rest of our lives. What a wild and beautiful paradox to live into!

- **Baptism, communion, and footwashing are signs of** God's work in us and in the world. They symbolize the Story of God's saving deeds in our world, especially in the life, death, and resurrection of Jesus. They are also signs of our response to the Story.

- **Baptism** represents God's action of forgiveness and salvation; it also marks our commitment to following Christ. Baptism is also associated with the coming of God's Spirit into our lives.

- **Communion is a sign of God's covenant** sealed in Jesus' death on the cross. It also is a sign of our participation in that new covenant.

- **We cannot follow Jesus alone.** When we declare our commitment to Jesus in baptism, we become part of the church—a family of faith where we can exercise our gifts and give and receive support for our faith journey.

What does it mean to be a disciple of Christ? Having started the journey, what are the next steps along the way? We'll look at these last questions in the next chapter—but take a few minutes to think about them now.

[2] Inspired by scholarly lectures by Marion Bontrager, Hesston College, Hesston, Kansas.

a **spiritual discipline** to practice:

Practice being church together. Get together with three to six others and commit to a time of sharing about your lives. To make things easier, have a bag of small household objects (picture, matches, pencil, comb, silk flower, eraser, etc.). Ask each person to pick one object to help him or her share, choosing one of these statements:

- I saw God this week when . . .
- The one miracle I would love to have is . . .
- If I could change one thing in my life right now . . .
- If I could change one thing in my church, it would be . . .
- I need your prayers for . . .

Topics in chapter 8

- **"Watering" the Christian life**
- **Spiritual disciplines**
- **Inner life**
- **Outer life**
- **Sharing good news**
- **Exercising spiritual gifts**

Story line:

Our own lives

8. Living into the Story

A good friend of mine once said, "Faith is like planting a tree in Kansas. Commitment is like watering it every day." I understand his point. Kansas is dry. It's windy. It's downright beastly hot in the summer. You can feel pretty idiotic about planting a tree in the middle of a prairie, where it seems like nothing but prairie dogs thrive. But while it might take some courage to plant the tree, it really takes gumption to water it—day after day after day.

If you have surrendered your life to Jesus and experienced baptism—or are planning to be baptized—you have "planted the tree." It took faith—as much faith, perhaps, as it takes to think a tree will grow on a prairie. But now that it's planted, what does it mean to "water" your new life? You have entered the Story. Now what does it mean to live into it?

Watering isn't always fun. But having a tree on the prairie is wonderful. Sometimes nurturing our life with God seems like hard work. But experiencing God is fabulous. In this chapter we'll discuss spiritual disciplines and the exercise of our spiritual gifts. Those are things that don't just happen; they require something of us. But as we cultivate and water, our Christian lives can be as satisfying as a cool drink of water on a hot summer day—under the shade of a huge tree.

There are Christians who do believe in God, do believe in the cross and everything, but for them it's all in the past. They just can't imagine God would actually talk to them or actually do something in the world today. —*Tara*

The early Christians had to learn how to water their faith.
People we read about in the book of Acts said yes to Jesus, were baptized, and became part of the church. But that was only the beginning. They experienced conversion, but the transformation wasn't done. Just like the disciples, these new believers had to learn to walk with Jesus. The problem *and* the advantage was that Jesus, no longer visible to the eye, was now experienced through the Holy Spirit. Sometimes that was very powerful and real (Acts 4:31), and at other times it took more faith than they seemed to have. That's why they kept meeting together for prayer, teaching, and support (Acts 4:32-34).

One telling story involves a teenager whose faith seemed further along than that of her elders. A group of believers were praying for Peter's delivery from prison. But when the prayer was actually answered and Peter showed up at the door, none of the believers could believe it—except Rhoda, a teenager. She kept insisting that the real Peter, not his ghost, was at the door. Finally, they checked themselves and let him in (Acts 12:6-17).

We don't have to, but we do have to. As it was for the early believers, so it is for us. When we become Christians, we become different. Jesus talks about our being "born again" (John 3:3 NIV), and Paul talks about God's people being a "new creation" (2 Cor 5:17). We gain a new identity. We do things that some people may think are crazy: we love our enemies and spend time in prayer because *not* to do them would be weird in God's scheme of things. How can we not do what is in our very nature to do?

Then the question is, "If the Holy Spirit is bringing all these changes now that I'm a Christian, what do I need to do?" Living the Christian life is hard to explain. The being and doing are all mixed up (James 2:14-26). On one hand, we don't have to do anything—period. We don't have to do things like praying and going to church. In fact, we *can't* do anything to win God's approval! God's love is a gift, and Christians call that undeserved love "grace."

On the other hand, if we have experienced God's grace, we find ourselves wanting to love God back through our lives. We find ourselves *wanting* to exercise spiritual disciplines and get our lives in line with God's will. So we'll do the work of watering and cultivating our faith, even when it's not glamorous. The simple discipline of going to church, for example, isn't absolutely wonderful all the time, but we understand that there is something beyond instant gratification here. Does that seem too far-fetched? Disciplines have a purpose and a joy beyond themselves. As Richard Foster writes in *The Celebration of Discipline*, they transform us. They make us effective for the journey of faith.

If God's gift of grace is real, it can also come dangerously close to what has been called "cheap grace." Cheap grace is when people think that they can live an undisciplined Christian life because God will always love and forgive them anyway.

Tara: May I be really, really honest? Sometimes I am like—who cares? I mean, I believe in God and everything, but I just go through the motions, play church, lah-de-dah. I felt pretty high that day I got baptized, but two weeks later—boom—same old, same old.

Mike: Isn't church a good thing?

Tara: Yes, it's a wonderful experience. I'm not being down on the church. I'm being down on pretending.

Rosella: Sometimes it *is* boring, and hard, but if you hold on to what you have in Jesus—it's wonderful.

Luke: Maybe, but we need to pay attention to this pretending thing.

Mike: Maybe the problem is that you accepted Jesus as Savior and not as Lord, too.

Tara: Ouch.

Mike: I'm sorry—

Tara: No—you're right, probably.

"**No one** may truly know
Christ, except one follows him
in life. And no one can follow
him, except he [or she] know
him." —*Hans Denck, early
Anabaptist leader*

Putting up the sails for God

Michele: Our Christian lives are like sailing a boat. We put up the sails so that we can catch the wind. The wind may or may not be blowing that day, so even though we put up our sails, we may not go very far. God is like the wind, and putting up the sails is like our spiritual disciplines. We can't force God's hand by putting up our sails, but if we don't spend time in prayer, for example, we won't catch the wind no matter how hard it blows (from Marjorie J. Thompson's *Soul Feast*; see page 180).

Mike: So you're saying we can't control God, but we can do things that prepare us for God.

Josh: So what in the world do you do when you can't do all the good stuff you are supposed to do?

Luke: I think you sit down in the middle of the floor and you say, "I give up," and maybe you cry, and—I don't know. For me, one of the biggest problems is trying to do the Christian life myself.

It's a control thing. Alone, we can't do what God calls us to do. But with the Holy Spirit, we can (Rom 7–8).

Rosella: We just have to relax in that grace.

Spiritual disciplines: habits of the heart

Mark Yaconelli, in his chapter in the book *Starting Right*, says, "Spiritual disciplines are the *means* through which believers seek to respond to God's invitations of love. They are the habits, disciplines, and patterns of life through which we seek communion with Christ and solidarity with others." The following is a list of habits and practices that help water the tree of our Christian life. Some are more central than others.

Prayer. Prayer is listening to God so much that we start to think God's thoughts and desire what God desires and love what God loves. Then, when we ask for something specific, which is our usual definition for prayer, God gives us what we ask for—because God has also given us the right desires (John 16:23-24; Ps 37:4).

The Lord's Prayer

Our Father in heaven,
hallowed be your name.
Your kingdom come.
Your will be done,
on earth as it is in heaven.
Give us this day our daily bread.
And forgive us our debts,
as we also have forgiven our debtors.
And do not bring us to the time of trial,
but rescue us from the evil one.
—*Matthew 6:9-13*

Michele: If God knows our hearts and is all-powerful, why do we even have to pray? Why doesn't God just take care of it?

Luke: Sometimes God does, right?

Michele: But why do we pray?

Luke: Maybe God wants us to be partners with God.

Josh: And why do we have to pray for things more than once? Why do we have to beg, which it almost seems like at times?

Rosella: Sometimes I have to pray for a long time, because the real thing that needs to be accomplished is for my will to become God's will. And I'm pretty stubborn.

Luke: So, does God answer prayer?

Mike: Yes. But sometimes God says no.

Mike: I can watch violent movies and not automatically go out and kill someone.

Luke: Yeah, but, little by little, doesn't it dehumanize certain groups of people for you? Doesn't it affect you just a little bit?

Tara: I know, I know. We should be thinking about whatever's good, whatever's pure, etc., etc. (Phil 4:8). But it's hard sometimes.

Michele: At what point do you trade the reality of the Story for the reality portrayed on the screen?

Bible study. God wants to replace old, destructive habits of thought with new life-giving habits. What we fill our minds with determines what kind of habits we form. God wants us to know—and live—and be changed by the Story. We study the Bible with an open heart and with others, for no one is so smart or so objective that they can discern the truth alone. In fact, arrogance is the death of this discipline. We study the Bible in its cultural and historical background so that we can understand the meaning it had for the original audience; then we apply it to our situation. We memorize Scripture so that the words become deeply ingrained in us.

Community worship. Just as much as we need alone time with God, we need time together with other believers. The early believers met daily to worship together (Acts 2:46). When we worship together in a local congregation, we can support each other, encourage each other, hold each other accountable.

Service. "If I, your Lord and Teacher, have washed your feet," Jesus told his disciples, "you also ought to wash one another's feet" (John 13:14). Service is the spiritual discipline whereby we "wash each other's feet." That may mean helping someone paint her house or volunteering in a homeless shelter. But it goes a lot deeper than outward actions. Ironically, the outward actions can be a stumbling block to true service. We can feel so good about what wonderful servants we are that we put ourselves above the ones we serve. True service helps us get rid of self-righteousness. True service helps us be humble. It breaks apart all pecking orders and dashes usual ideas of leadership.

Simplicity. Simplicity sets possessions in their proper place. It's not that things are bad in and of themselves; it's just that they're not God. Simplicity is really an inward reality—seeking God's kingdom first and finding true joy there. That results in the outward reality of being free from worry over materialistic things. You can take them or leave them (Phil 4:10-11).

The discipline of simplicity also speaks to us about our use of time. Our schedules can get so busy we hardly have time for anything other than endless work! What does that say about where we are putting our ultimate trust? What freedom is there when we are slaves to our schedules? As Richard Foster has said, the purpose of spiritual disciplines is freedom—freedom from the enslaving habits of sin, freedom to be mature in Christ, freedom to place ourselves before God so that God can transform us.

Josh: So is simplicity the way we keep money from becoming our god?

Mike: Whatever we put our securities in, that is our god, so yes.

Tara: But if you put simplicity on a pedestal, can't it become a god, too? Or a slave-master? What I mean is, you can get really oppressive with this voluntary poverty stuff. Or am I just reacting to my own guilt?

Luke: Do material things rule your life?

Tara: I don't know.

Michele: You have to focus on the kingdom or all these disciplines get legalistic—and bad news.

Rosella: But there is so much joy in sharing your money and food with others who need it. God always, always provides for our needs. Our possessions are really God's anyway.

Tara: We can think we're not owned by our possessions and living in simplicity but really be fooling ourselves.

Josh: Isn't tithing and giving offerings to God part of all this, too? I think when we give our money—God's money—back to God, we can help make sure money isn't our god.

Fasting. Fasting is the discipline of refraining from something—usually food—in order to focus more directly on God. The Israelites would fast for two reasons: to repent, usually as an entire nation (Joel 2; Esther 4), and to prepare themselves for receiving the spiritual strength to complete a hard task. Jesus fasted in the wilderness (Matt 4:1-11; see also Exod 24 and 34, 1 Kings 19). When we go without food and get hungry, we begin to realize our dependence on God. It breaks the rhythm of life. It creates enough disequilibrium (weirdness) in our lives that we become more sensitive to God's quiet voice speaking to us.

Silence and solitude. Many Christians practice spending time alone, without talking or other distractions for a specific amount of time. This quiet time creates a space for God to speak to them. Rather than loneliness, solitude brings an inner fullness that is actually the best medicine for loneliness. We can't run away from ourselves anymore, and when we can finally face ourselves—with God to help us, the joy is overflowing.

Journaling. Journaling is writing our prayers and thoughts out on paper. More than a diary and not quite an essay, journaling helps us reflect on God, listen, and sort out what God is trying to say to us.

Confession. If we realize God loves us even though we mess up, we can bear to admit and repent of our sins. If we don't examine our lives as part of being a healthy Christian, we will tend to blame others when it really is our fault. We will make excuses that keep us from finding the freedom from sin that we need. So we do examine our lives, sometimes with the help of others, to figure all this out. We confess our part of the mess. With the help of the Holy Spirit, we change our behavior. And through all of this, we feel God's love.

Forgiveness. The other side of confession is forgiveness. Others have hurt us. Now the bondage is not only the pain of our hurt, but also the anger we feel toward those who have hurt us. So to work toward freedom and healing we must either forgive them, or "for-grieve" them (to borrow a phrase from David Augsburger's book *Helping People Forgive*).

If the person who hurt us recognizes his or her fault and confesses it to us, we must forgive that person. God has forgiven us, and, as the Lord's Prayer reminds us, we experience God's forgiveness as we forgive others. As Jesus instructed, we are to forgive "seventy times seven" (Matt 18:21-34).

When the wrongdoer is not willing or not available to confess, we must "for-grieve" him or her. In doing so, we release those hurts to God, we ask for healing, and we move on with our lives. This

---

Living it out

Struggling with forgiveness: I have experienced plenty of trials in the realm of hurt and forgiveness in the past 20 years. Growing up with an abusive, present but still "absentee" father, I learned at a very early age what it meant to hate someone enough to pray for his death. I loved myself and my family too much to ever actually conspire to kill him. I left that up to God.

As I accepted Christ into my life and learned to walk with him, I really struggled with Christianity's emphasis on forgiveness. I could not forgive or forget what my dad had put my family through, especially because, after all of these years, he never would admit he ever did anything wrong. I still have never heard him say, "I am sorry" or "I was wrong." I get to a point where I feel compassion and love for him and I feel sorry for him, but then he does something painful and the cycle begins all over.

I have struggled with the concept of forgiveness. How can I forgive him if he never repents? I am working on giving all this to God. That's easier said than done, but I'm at a better place than I used to be.
—*Anonymous*

should be done only after we have attempted to be reconciled with the other person as much as possible. In this way, we have done our part to work at forgiveness and reconciliation, and we are not bound by the slavery of our angry feelings.

Even when people do ask for our forgiveness, sometimes the hurt goes so deep that it takes many years for us to really forgive. That's okay, as long as we are working at it with God's help. God is with us—each step of the way.

What spiritual disciplines have you made a habit in your life? Which ones would you like to do better?

Practicing the disciplines. These disciplines are the most common, but there are others, such as spiritual guidance, intercession, hospitality, and submission. Some, such as prayer, Bible reading, and forgiveness, are pretty essential. Others, such as journaling, depend on our personalities and are optional. Whichever ones we choose, we will be most healthy in our Christian lives if we keep a balance in three areas: being alone with God, connecting with other believers in the church, and serving in the world beyond ourselves.

How do you keep the practices of the Christian life from becoming ends in themselves rather than means to grow in your relationship with God?

Each of us may have a slightly different mix of disciplines and practices. But all of us are called—all of the time—to let God transform us. Being a Christian means living differently from the rest of the world, letting God shape our values. Our salvation affects our ethics—our sense of what's right and wrong. We treat our families with respect and love. We live according to the Bible's high standards for sexual purity. We don't cheat on tests. We don't gossip or spread lies. We care about and befriend unpopular kids in school. Why? Because we are God's people and because we are in Christ and because our whole identity has changed. We are different. And it shows.

Words and deeds that attract others to Jesus. Because we are different, people around us will take note. When they hear the Story, including how we entered into it, they will be curious. When they see how we are being transformed to be like Christ (1 Cor 2:16), they may want that transformation, too. When they hear how we experience God in prayer and see how we love our enemies, they may say, "count me in." That is why Peter writes that every Christian should be prepared to give an answer to everyone who asks you to give the reason for the hope that you have (1 Pet 3:15). See the Confession of Faith summary of Article 10 on page 175 for the importance we place on mission.

> *ethics:* principles of human conduct, with respect to the rightness or wrongness of actions and the goodness and badness of motives and ends

God's people—from Old Testament times to today—are called to spread God's good news to an ever-widening circle (Matt 28:19-20). This is evangelism—sharing the good news of Jesus and inviting others to begin a relationship with Jesus. We share the good news with others because we are experiencing it ourselves and are able to recommend it to others. When that happens, we're seeing the Story advance. Abraham and Sarah were told they would be a blessing to all the people of the earth. Today God wants to bless others through us.

Michele: How do we interact with culture enough that they will listen to us tell about God's love?

Luke: We need to meet people where they're at.

Josh: We need to admit that we are every bit a part of culture as the next guy.

Mike: So would you go to a party where there's drinking so you could be friends with someone who needs Jesus?

Josh: Why not? But would you drink with them?

Mike: No. Where do you draw the line?

Josh: You have to draw the line when you are compromising your morals and beliefs.

Mike: But there are other things just as bad as drinking. What about cheating on your income tax or overeating or overworking? That's not trusting God. What about having nice things while other people starve to death?

Josh: Okay, so we are back to syncretism. We probably consume too much because we have bought into the values—even though they aren't specifically a pagan religion—that we need stuff. Yet the Bible says something different than that.

Luke: I think worshiping God means something different than that.

Discovering your spiritual gifts

What is a spiritual gift that you are discovering or exercising? How do you work at finding out what gifts God has called you to use for God's kingdom?

Everyone who says yes to Jesus has a mission. Every new believer—just like Abraham, Lydia, and Barnabas—gets a supernatural tap on the shoulder and a voice in the ear saying, "Have I got a job for you!" The apostle Paul writes about the church as a body in which each part, each organ, has a unique role (1 Cor 12:12-26). Paul calls these jobs "gifts"—abilities from the Holy Spirit that help build up God's people and get God's work done in the world.

In 1 Corinthians 12, Ephesians 4, and Romans 12, Paul lists several of those jobs as he talks about the work of the church. Putting those lists together, the jobs include serving as apostles, prophets, evangelists, pastors, or teachers; compassion; exhortation; giving; leadership; speaking in tongues; interpreting tongues; healing; miracle-working; faith; and discernment of spirits (see Rom 12:5-8; 1 Cor 12:8-11; Eph 4:11-16). All of these—and many others—help to build up the church until everyone comes to unity, maturity, and "the measure of the full stature of Christ" (Eph 4:13).

Spiritual gifts come with a few cautions. First, your gift is not for you. It is for the church (Eph 4:12) and for the continuation of God's Story in our world. Second, all gifts in the church are different, yet equally important. When Paul compared the Corinthian church to a human body, he emphasized that diversity was good; not everyone can be an "eye." And every gift in the church was needed, just as a body needs each part; what would we do without a nose?

Third, unless the gifts are exercised in love, they are useless (1 Cor 13). Paul had to get right in the faces of some church members who thought they were hot-stuff spiritual giants because of their gifts. Ironically, the more arrogant they got, the more they showed how spiritually immature they really were.

Fourth, we can be too timid about using our gifts. Some Christians look at their young age or their lack of experience and education and they think, Wow, I can't do that. But God is not necessarily concerned with age or education. God wants people who are available and want to serve God. As Richard Foster says in *Celebration of Discipline*, a longing for God is the primary requirement for practicing the disciplines and using our gifts.

Like Mary, who was asked at a young age to be the mother of Jesus, we each have a calling. Like Paul's young coworker, Timothy, we are each called to serve, knowing that the one who made the blind see is the same one working in and through us. God can and does work through each one who says yes to Jesus—sometimes in miraculous ways, other times in low-key ways.

It can be difficult to really believe that God does want to use us. But God does. We know this through the Story. The Story tells us that God wants to interact with us, whether through our spiritual

---

Mike: As soon as we commit to God, don't the temptations come rolling in even more? Maybe it's not supposed to be fun and games.

Luke: Then why do it? Why have a relationship with God if there are no benefits?

Rosella: There are benefits. Our sins are forgiven, and we go to heaven for eternity.

Luke: Yes, and maybe I should be more grateful for all that. But it seems sometimes like God is the big Candy Guy, who has really good stuff. Pray just right and God has to give you what you want. See, I want . . . something more.

Rosella: Oh yes, there is something more—God's love, the guidance of the Spirit, the peace . . .

Mike: But what if you don't have those things?

Rosella: Just because you don't feel those things doesn't mean you don't have those things.

Tara: But how do you know you have them if you don't feel them? . . . I guess that's faith.

Michele: Following Jesus is the absolutely hardest thing you'll ever do and the most joyous thing you'll ever do all at the same time.

Mike: It's a relationship.

Michele: It's a relationship—a real one, whether it feels like it or not.

disciplines or through our gifts, so that we can experience more of God. In some ways, it's a double whammy. Every day, every hour, we must look for God, expect God, listen and watch for God. At the same time, we believe in God even when we don't feel a thing and there seems to be no evidence that God is even around.

See the Confession of Faith summary of Article 17 on page 176 about discipleship.

It's like watering a tree. You can't see the tree growing. Day after day it looks just like a little twig. But you keep watering, and suddenly one day you realize it's on its way to being a giant oak tree. How did it happen? Your watering every day did not make the tree grow—God did. But by watering it, you helped provide the environment where it could grow. As we practice the disciplines, and as we practice using our spiritual gifts, our faith grows. We are transformed. We experience God in ever new and wonderful ways.

Summing it up:

- **As Christians, we practice spiritual disciplines.** There are many ways of explaining why we do so, but it comes down to this: we are followers of Jesus Christ. We nurture and deepen that relationship as we practice life-giving habits. We water the tree, and it grows healthy and strong.

- **Our salvation impacts our behavior.** Every day, in big and small ways, we live differently because of Jesus. By the way we live, we reflect who we are and who we are becoming in Christ.

- **We represent God to others.** God depends on Christians to announce to others, in words and deeds, the good news that God loves the world and offers healing and hope.

- **We are given spiritual gifts to help us live out our unique mission in life.** The Holy Spirit gives us spiritual gifts, which we in turn use to help build God's kingdom. Most often other Christians in the local church help us discern what our gifts are.

- **The Story continues.** The Story didn't end with the early church. God still wants to draw people from every walk of life into the people of God. How that has happened over the years and how the Mennonites fit into the Story is our next topic for discussion.

How do you feel about sharing your faith story with friends, especially those who are not Christian?

a **spiritual discipline** to practice:

One of the basic and needed spiritual disciplines is the practice of silence. Grab some paper and a pen, and take one hour just to be by yourself. Don't allow yourself a cell phone or any electronic device. If weather permits, spend the hour outdoors. Write down whatever comes to your mind. If nothing comes to your mind, just enjoy the rest and the quiet. Give yourself the grace of low expectations. Just waste time with God.

Topics in chapter 9

- **The church through the centuries**
- **The Anabaptists**
  Mennonites today
- **The difference between Anabaptists and other Christians**
- **The future end of the Story**
- **The Story continues in our lives**

Story line:
The church through the centuries
New heavens and new earth (Revelation)

9. The Rest of the Story

It's wild to think we are part of God's working in the world.
Christians are part of something very big—the church. It's more than
any denomination, such as Mennonite, Lutheran, or Roman Catholic.
All those who have said yes to the Story and live in the Story—all
God's people throughout the world and throughout history—are part
of it. And the Story continues to unfold today.

During every period of the church's history, faithful Christians
have kept the Story moving. Two hundred years after the resurrection
of Jesus, Christians faced gladiators in Rome because of their faith.
A thousand years after the resurrection, some gave up everything to
devote their lives to prayer and helping the poor. Fifteen hundred
years after the resurrection, others were being executed for their
commitment to follow Jesus and remain true to the Bible. Today, the
Christian faith keeps attracting others, even in countries where the
culture is hostile to Christians.

Even though the Story has continued on for more than 2,000
years, the same issues have been at the heart of the faith. What does
it mean to follow Jesus? Who is truly Lord of our lives? What does it
mean to be part of the world and yet be citizens of God's kingdom?
How should the church function in relationship to the state?

Sometimes it's hard to remember that I am a part of something so much bigger than I am. I'm part of the people of God, millions strong. —*Tara*

The answers to these questions have never been easy, but the story of the church over the years can help us in working with them. We look at the lives of Christians from other ages and other countries not to copy exactly what they did, but to take lessons from them as we carry the Story in our own lives. With the help of the Spirit, we can not only learn what it means to be faithful, but also have the courage to live it out. Let's look at how the Story has been lived out since Jesus' time.

Two thousand years of Christianity in a nutshell

The first 300 years. Until the fourth century after Christ, Christians met mainly in each other's homes. They shared their possessions freely, cared for the poor among them, and welcomed everyone no matter who they were or where they came from. They were nonviolent, refusing to mistreat their personal enemies and refusing to fight in the Roman army.

During this time, Christian leaders and scholars began to write down their understandings about God and Jesus to guard against teachers and philosophies that corrupted Christian faith. They laid the groundwork for decisions about which documents—Gospels, letters, and other writings—had enough authority to be included in our Bible.

Find out about the persecution of Christians today. Do an Internet search to learn about people who face great hardship because they follow God.

Mike: So the early church was perfect?

Michele: No, but what they did in those early years showed the shalom God wanted way back in the wilderness. Only this time—I think because of the Holy Spirit and the example of Jesus—it could work better.

Luke: So why don't we live like that?

Josh: Some Christians do.

These first three centuries, however, were also difficult for the church. Because Christians called Jesus their Lord, rather than Caesar, they experienced waves of persecution. Sometimes Christians were thrown to the lions, sometimes crucified or burned on poles along the Roman roads. Persecution scattered the Christian movement farther throughout the known parts of the world. It also made them stronger in their faith. By the end of the second century, the church often required new believers to take long periods of prebaptism instruction (often three years) in order to make sure they were ready for possible suffering. Despite great opposition, the church grew in number. As an early church leader, Tertullian said, "the blood of the martyrs was the seed of the church."

Constantine. All this changed with Emperor Constantine in 313 CE. He was fighting in a battle when he saw a vision of a shining cross in the sky. He heard a voice say, "In this symbol, conquer." He told God that if he won the battle, he would become a Christian. He did win, and there was soon a total turnaround in the treatment of Christians. Through the Edict of Milan, the emperor now called for the toleration of all religions. It was only a short step until another emperor, Theodosius, made Christianity the *only* religion allowed.

At first glance, this seemed like good news—no more being fed to the lions. But Constantine's idea of making society Christian through the power of the state was almost the death of the church. Now people were forced into being Christians, or they were considered Christians because of their nationality. As the church became "official," many Christians didn't even know that being a Christian meant living a transformed life, free from sin. Choosing to follow Jesus in obedient love wasn't even on the radar screen.

For Christians . . . do not live somewhere in cities of their own, or use some distinctive language, or practice a peculiar manner of life. Though they . . . follow local customs in dress and food and the rest of their living, their own way of life which they display is wonderful and admittedly strange. . . . They take part in everything like citizens, and endure everything like aliens. . . . like everyone else they marry, they have children, but not a common bed. . . . they remain on earth, but they are citizens of heaven.

—*from correspondence of a Christian between 150 and 180 CE*

Tara: Actually, Constantine's action wasn't that new. The Israelites in the Old Testament made the same mistake when they established their monarchy. When they combined worship of God with citizenship in their nation, they were putting God in a box.

Luke: Jesus faced the same kind of temptation, right? Become a great political leader, use the official power of the state, and they won't kill you.

The centuries that followed were known as the Middle Ages. The Roman Empire crumbled, and yet the church continued to enjoy great power. In 1054, the one church became two—the Roman Church (Catholic) and the Eastern Church (Orthodox), both claiming to be the real church. The head of the Roman Catholic Church, the pope, often had more power over the state than emperors or kings. As the church gained more land, it soon became very wealthy. Rich people thought they could buy their own forgiveness from sin by contributing to the church.

Soldiers went to the Middle East on a mission called the Crusades to recapture the Holy Land from the Muslim Turks. While some went with good intentions, many others went to gain wealth and have adventure. In the name of Christ, thousands of innocent people—Muslims, Jews, and Eastern Christians—were plundered, killed, or "converted" at the point of a sword.

Monk copying Scriptures by hand

All was not bad in the Middle Ages, however. Monks and nuns who wanted to live out the teachings of Jesus lived together in community. They remained unmarried and became voluntarily poor so that they could devote themselves to prayer and service. They fed the hungry and cared for the sick. They copied the Scriptures from ancient texts. In many ways, they tried to bring the church back to what it was in the beginning.

The Reformation. By the 1500s, an incredible revolution was forming in Western Europe. Explorers from other lands brought new ideas. People rediscovered ancient writings, which made them question traditional religious ideas. Christian reformers like John Hus and John Wycliff called for common people to study the Bible for themselves. A man named Johann Gutenberg invented the printing press, which made it possible for people to get books at affordable prices, including the Bible. With all these changes it became more and more difficult for the state or the church to control what people believed and taught.

The printing press

Enter Martin Luther. This German monk, like so many others, was disturbed about the state of the church. He was especially bothered by the way spiritual favors were sold by an ever-richer Roman church. In 1517, Luther wrote a stinging criticism of the state church and nailed it on the door of the church in Wittenburg. Arguing from the Bible, which he eventually translated into German, Luther preached that people are made right with God through faith, not by their efforts to please God or by the rituals of the church. Because of such protest, the movement Luther began was called the Protestant Reformation. The term *Protestant* still applies to non-Catholic denominations today.

The hierarchy of the Roman church bitterly opposed Luther, but several powerful princes who agreed with his teaching protected him. His reforms were able to thrive in Germany and spread to other parts of Europe. Luther worked to give the new movement political power, so that the reformed churches would become state churches just as the Roman Catholic Church had been. Ironically, after these reformers gained their own religious freedom, they denied that freedom to others.

Martin Luther

Ulrich Zwingli of Zurich, Switzerland, was one such reformer. He went further than other thinkers of his day, daring to think of a church that could be somewhat free from the state. He even

Ulrich Zwingli

Conrad Grebel —O. W. Schenk

Felix Manz —O. W. Schenk

Georg Blaurock —O. W. Schenk

questioned the traditional practice of baptizing babies. But the government authorities of Zurich put pressure on Zwingli not to go too far in his reforms. Apparently infant baptism was still the best way to have a head count of citizens for tax purposes. Zwingli soon buckled and kept the link between church and state strong.

The Anabaptists. Several of Zwingli's followers did not buckle. Conrad Grebel, Felix Manz, and Georg Blaurock refused to compromise what they clearly understood from the Bible. They were convinced that the only way to experience the true church was to join God's people because you wanted to, not because you were born into it. They knew that membership in the church based on membership in the state was no real Christianity at all. Grebel and the others argued these points vigorously with the government officials, and they refused to have their own babies baptized.

At a meeting in January 1525, Grebel baptized Blaurock, and Blaurock in turn baptized Grebel and several others present with them. In that simple act, they defied their government and the state church, returning to the free churches of the time before Constantine. They, and thousands of other likeminded believers after them, began to meet informally as an alternative church. They also went everywhere, calling others to a personal commitment to Jesus.

These believers paid a heavy price for their actions. People made fun of them by calling them Anabaptists ("again-baptizers," since the first members had already been baptized as babies). The governments of Europe, both Catholic and Protestant, outlawed the movement, forcing the Anabaptists to meet secretly in homes and in forests. Thousands were tortured, run through with a sword, drowned, or burned at the stake. But despite the bloody persecution, the Anabaptist movement spread like wildfire through Switzerland, Germany, Holland, and other countries in Eastern and Western Europe.

Though there were variations among the different groups of Anabaptists, Michael Sattler and other leaders hammered out seven important beliefs they could agree upon. They called it the Schleitheim Confession. Its main points follow:

- The rejection of infant baptism as a means of salvation

- Keeping the church pure by banning members who had strayed from their commitment and refused to change (see Matt 18:15-20; this was in contrast to the state, which used violent physical punishment for breaking church or state rules)

- The Lord's Supper as a memorial of the Lord's death, not as a ritual where the bread and wine actually become Christ's body and blood (as the Catholic church believed)

- Separation from the world's values

- Lay people as congregational pastors and leaders

- Nonresistance, including the refusal to bear arms

- Forbidding the swearing of oaths

What beliefs would you die for?

Menno Simons. One of the most important leaders of the Anabaptists was a man from Holland named Menno Simons. Menno began his career as a Catholic priest. For years, he struggled with many doubts about the state church's practices. Even more, he was bothered that his fellow church leaders based their beliefs on church tradition, not the Bible.

At that time, some Anabaptists in Germany adopted some bizarre beliefs, including the use of violent force to establish their movement. In 1536, after hearing about these misguided beliefs, Menno knew

Menno Simons —A. Hendricks

True evangelical faith cannot lie dormant. It clothes the naked. It feeds the hungry. It comforts the sorrowful. It shelters the destitute. It serves those that harm it. It binds up that which is wounded. It has become all things to all people. —*Menno Simons, 1539*

Anneken Hendriks, burned in Amsterdam in 1571

From *Martyrs Mirror*, 1938, Herald Press. Illustration by Jan Luyken

that he must leave the state church and join the peaceful Anabaptists. Soon he became a recognized leader of the Anabaptists. Always stressing the importance of interpreting Scriptures through the life of Christ, he helped them distinguish truth from wrong teaching. Eventually, many Anabaptists became known as "Mennonites."

Mennonites—on the move until today

Intense persecution of Anabaptists continued through the 16th and early 17th centuries. Eventually they settled into close-knit communities where they could practice their faith in peace. Often because of their refusal to join the military or bear arms, Mennonites had to migrate to countries or regions where service was optional. They migrated to many parts of Europe, the Ukraine, and North and South America. Sometimes they moved because they were directly persecuted and in danger for their faith.

North America became a refuge for Mennonites from the persecution and rising militarism of Europe. At the invitation of William Penn, a group of 34 Mennonites and Quakers from Germany arrived in America in 1683 after a 10-week journey across the ocean. Settling in Germantown, Pennsylvania, this group made the first formal protest against the slavery system in America. Soon, thousands of other Mennonites, primarily from Switzerland and South Germany, moved to Pennsylvania and then on to Ohio, Indiana, and further west. Others went north to Ontario.

From the beginning, the Mennonites lived among other groups of people. They did not have their own land reserve as Mennonites in Russia did (see below). So they had to figure out how to relate to people who believed differently than they did and at the same time preserve what they believed in. Many chose to isolate themselves from the wider culture by dressing differently and speaking their European languages. In the United States, the Revolutionary War of 1776 and the Civil War of 1861 were testing times for the Mennonites, but also opportunities to strengthen their faith. The Civil War forced the Mennonites to rethink their teaching on nonresistance. Many suffered persecution for not serving in the military.

The Mennonites who went to Russia to escape persecution have an especially moving story. Beginning in the 1780s, Mennonites moved to the Ukraine and made prosperous colonies there. The Russian government gave them much freedom, including religious freedom and exemption from military duty. But within a hundred years, those freedoms started fading. When the Bolshevik Revolution came in 1917, the colonies were in true danger. They were attacked by armies on both sides and by others jealous of their wealth. Famine struck. Hundreds of Mennonites died. Many were able to flee to Canada and the U.S., but many others were forced to stay. Some were sent to Siberia where they faced forced labor, cold, and hunger. During World War II, many Russian Mennonites were able to flee to

My great-grandfather had to choose between serving in the army and being tarred and feathered. He understood that it was the government's right to punish him, but he trusted God to take care of him. One afternoon, men came with buckets of hot tar. When they got about three feet away from him, they stopped in their tracks, gave out a cry, dropped their buckets, and ran. No one knows for sure what they saw or why they ran. But my great-grandfather believed that God protected him that day. —*Michele*

Mennonite refugees aboard the *S. S. Volendam* on their way to Paraguay from Europe in 1948

Mennonite Central Committee Collection, Mennonite Church USA Archives.

Europe, then went on to settle in North America and several countries in South America.

Even in our generation, many Mennonites are under pressure from their societies and governments. In 1982, the Ethiopian Mennonite Church, known as Meserete Kristos (Christ the Foundation), was outlawed by the Marxist government. They had to go underground, suffering intense persecution for nine years. But God blessed this time of hiding and persecution. When religious freedom was granted again in 1991, Meserete Kristos realized that they now numbered 50,000, a tenfold increase.

Mennonites in mission. In the late 1800s, Mennonites in North America, Russia, and Holland began to look outward again. Like many other Christian groups, they felt a new call to fulfill Jesus' last instructions to his disciples to make disciples of all nations (Matt 28:19). Missionaries started churches in Indonesia, India, Congo, China, Argentina, Colombia, Ethiopia, and many other countries. As they shared the good news of Christ, they also served human need by establishing hospitals, schools, orphanages, and economic development programs. Mennonite denominations in North America began banding together to do relief and development work through organizations such as Mennonite Central Committee, Mennonite Disaster Service, and Mennonite Economic Development Associates.

Especially in the last half of the 20th century, Mennonites also began planting churches in North American cities, attracting people from a wide variety of ethnic backgrounds. Today there are thriving African-American and Hispanic Mennonite churches, as well as other-language congregations of immigrants. A small but significant group of Mennonites are in French-speaking Quebec. The

Michele: There's a dilemma here. Sometimes in our history we have been so good at mission. At other times, we have been little stick-to-our-own-kind communities.

Rosella: Hasn't every denomination done that to a certain extent?

Josh: We've often been the "quiet in the land" and have not reached out.

Luke: It's really hard to reach out to people when you're being persecuted.

Tara: But we're not being persecuted right now.

stereotype that many North Americans have had of Mennonites—German-origin folks who keep to themselves—has been steadily breaking down.

By the 1960s a worldwide network of Mennonite churches was coming into being; this network became known as the Mennonite World Conference. More and more, the new churches no longer saw themselves just as daughter churches of North America and Europe. They now became the ones who "made disciples" in their own communities and beyond. The church continued to grow in numbers, especially in India, Congo, Indonesia, and Ethiopia. At the year 2000, there were one million members worldwide in 60 countries; more than half were from countries outside of Europe and North America.

Although there is still lots of room to become more faithful, it is awesome to think that in some small way the Mennonite Church is part of God's ancient promise to Abraham and Sarah: that through them "all the nations of the earth will be blessed." Who could have imagined?

Rosella: For all of us around this table, this is our story as Anabaptists.

Mike: But not all my ancestors came from Switzerland or Russia.

Tara: That's not the point. Do you believe in believers baptism?

Mike: Yes.

Tara: Then you're in. You're an Anabaptist.

Josh: Well now, there's more to it than that. You have to follow Jesus and everything.

Luke: But the point Tara is making is that the story isn't about an ethnic group; it is about anybody who wants to follow Jesus in the way Anabaptists do. I'm African-American, I'm not blood-related to Conrad Grebel, but hey, I'm an Anabaptist Mennonite as much as anyone else.

Tara: It's not something you're born into. It's something you choose.

Living it out

The Stolen Tools: My heart was singing as I traced outlines of donated tools on the workshop wall of our Church Community Centre: six hammers, six saws, six of everything needed to build interesting projects. Not only were the tools now available for our woodworking classes for kids living below the poverty line, but each tool could be returned easily to its designated spot, encouraging good management.

Entering the Centre one morning all I could do was stare. The wall with its organized, chalked-out shapes was bare. Every precious tool was missing! I was angry! Let's call the police and get these troublemakers put into jail! Let's cancel our neighborhood program, if that's what people will do!

In our staff meeting a few days earlier, we had looked at the creation story. It had dawned on us that even though people make bad choices, one can never take away one vital factor—that every person is created in the image of God and therefore has some good qualities.

Reflecting more deeply on this study, a thought occurred to me. I put a notice in the local community newsletter calling for the tools to be returned for the benefit of the neighborhood—no questions asked.

Within a few days almost every tool was back in its place. A young man who was staying out of trouble but still on probation had persuaded the guilty ones to reconsider their actions. —*Doreen and Hugo Neufeld, Calgary, Alberta*

What's the difference between Anabaptists and other Christians?

Anabaptists today—including Mennonites—generally accept the core beliefs that other Christians have held for centuries. The Apostles' Creed is an ancient summary of those beliefs (see sidebar). But ever since the Schleitheim Confession (see page 155). Anabaptists have stated their distinct beliefs in various ways. One reference point today for members of Mennonite Church Canada and Mennonite Church USA, for example, is the *Confession of Faith in a Mennonite Perspective*, which is summarized on pages 173–177. Here is a summary of the differences between Anabaptists and others:

The Apostles' Creed

I believe in God, the Father almighty, creator of heaven and earth.

I believe in Jesus Christ, God's only Son, our Lord, who was conceived by the Holy Spirit, born of the Virgin Mary, suffered under Pontius Pilate, was crucified, died, and was buried; he descended to the dead. On the third day he rose again; he ascended into heaven, he is seated at the right hand of the Father, and he will come again to judge the living and the dead.

I believe in the Holy Spirit, the holy catholic church, the communion of saints, the forgiveness of sins, the resurrection of the body, and the life everlasting. Amen.

Michele: The Anabaptists would have added one thing to the Apostles' Creed—the life and teachings of Jesus.

Believers baptism. Most Christian churches baptize babies who later "confirm" their faith publicly after a period of instruction. Anabaptists believe the Bible teaches that baptism should follow a person's decision to follow Jesus. Children cannot make that decision, and are safe in God's care until they can. When they can understand and make choices about their spiritual lives, children enter what we call the "age of accountability." Believers make a public commitment to follow Jesus, and that is evident in how they live their lives. That is why Anabaptists value the idea of a "visible church."

Jesus is the standard for our Christian living. Many Christians emphasize the importance of having the right set of beliefs or rituals. Anabaptists believe that following Jesus is at the heart of our faith. When in doubt about what is the right thing to do, we look at what Jesus did and taught as our standard. It's true that some of the things Jesus asks us to do seem impossible—like loving our enemies. But we believe that with the Spirit's help we are called to live the life he taught.

Our faith is both public and private. Some Christians believe that we can divide our lives in two—private and public. In their private lives, they follow Jesus. But in their public lives, their top responsibility goes to the government or to their job. For example, if the state asks them to fight in an army, they do it. If they accept Jesus' call to love enemies, that is reserved for the private side of life. Anabaptists believe that the same ethics apply Monday and Sunday, in public and private.

The church is a living community of God's new people. In some Christian traditions, the church is a place for individuals to hear the word, worship, and receive the rites of the church from religious professionals. Anabaptists say that *all* members share in the church's work. We use our spiritual gifts to build up the church. We know that by ourselves we won't hear God perfectly, and we won't have the strength to live out our calling. That's why we submit ourselves to one another for correction and support. In the church we care enough about each other to speak the truth in love, confessing our faults and forgiving each other. We don't just leave when things don't go our way. We know we need each other.

Luke: I'm sensing another paradox. For a church community to really work, we need to care enough to hold each other accountable, even confronting each other when we're not living the life God calls us to. But that only works if we love each other enough to be loyal, no matter what.

Josh: If I thought my church family was going to reject me, I wouldn't bring up any controversial topics.

Tara: Or even doubts or questions I had.

Luke: Exactly. But the opposite is true, too. We have to care enough about each other to critique each other—in love.

God calls us to work for peace and justice. Some Christians believe that in certain circumstances, God is in favor of using violence to achieve goals. Anabaptists disagree. If Jesus' life and teaching are our standard, and if we are truly empowered by the Spirit to live like Jesus did, then living nonviolently and working for the shalom of all people are the natural outcomes. That is why Mennonites not only oppose war, but also work to take away the conditions—such as poverty and oppression—that cause violence and war. We do not believe, as some Christians do, that God really cares only about spiritual salvation. We are called to feed the hungry, clothe the naked, and visit those in prison out of the heartfelt love that flows out of us . . . just like Jesus did.

The Bible is the highest authority. All of the points above rest on how we view the Bible. Most Christian denominations (including Anabaptists) affirm that the Bible is their highest authority (2 Tim 3:16). The Scriptures are inspired by God, and can be trusted completely for our faith and life (Prov 30:5). More than many other denominations, however, Anabaptists emphasize that the Scriptures

---

Tips on using the Bible

1) Don't cut and paste, taking verses out of their context. Read each passage in light of the whole Story.

2) Use the story of Jesus as the measuring stick in figuring out what the Bible says. When in doubt ask, "What would Jesus do?"

3) Obey what is already clear. An elderly Mennonite pastor once said, "If you don't understand Scripture, obey what is already clearly spelled out—like feeding the poor, loving all people. Doing this will help you figure out the rest."

4) Find out about the culture and history of the time when the Bible was written.

5) Ask others. Studying the Bible in community helps us all learn.

6) Pray. Jesus promised that the Holy Spirit would guide us into truth (John 16:13).

should be interpreted "Christocentrically." That is, we believe that Jesus Christ is the clearest picture of God, and of what God's ultimate will is for us (Heb 1:1-3; John 1:14, 18). So when the Bible seems to give us different messages about a certain topic (like war), we look at what Jesus says first and interpret everything else in light of Jesus.

What will the future hold?

While it's anyone's guess as to what the church will look like 10 years from now, the Bible gives us some idea of what will happen to the church—and the world—at the end of time. Jesus promised that he would come again in victory. Paul and the other New Testament writers clearly show the early church's conviction that Jesus will come again and that believers should be ready. And when Christ comes again, God will make all things right in the world. That will be the grand finale to God's Story and our story. Here are a few things the Bible points out:

The reign of God has already begun. When Jesus started his work, his main message was "The kingdom of God has come near; repent, and believe in the good news" (Mark 1:15). In his teaching he

---

Michele: What do you think the church will look like in 10 years?

Tara: We won't care about all the rules so much.

Luke: But, hopefully, we will be so overwhelmed with the love of Jesus that we will just draw all sorts of people and they won't be turned away by our high standards.

Tara: High standards that won't be mandatory?

Luke: Yeah, I mean, it's the grace and holiness thing again.

emphasized that the reign of God is here among us (Luke 17:20-21). One of the paradoxes of Christianity is that while the reign of God will come to full realization at the end of the ages (see below), it is already here. As one theologian put it, God's rule is "already" but "not yet" at the same time.

Jesus will return to earth. Jesus spoke of his return often (Matt 24–25; Mark 13; John 14–17), and the angel confirmed it when Jesus returned to heaven (Acts 1:11). When he comes, it will not be like his first coming as a small baby, when only a few recognized him. Jesus will come in might and honor (Acts 1:11; Matt 24:30; see also Dan 7:9-14).

It will not be a victory of military might, but of truth and justice. The book of Revelation depicts a final war against evil and against Satan (Rev 19:11-16). Like many other things in the book, however, this war is symbolic. Jesus appears as the "Word of God," and the only weapon he has is a sharp sword coming out of his mouth—a symbol of the word of God (Eph 6:17). The God who created the world with a mighty word will come again and bring back order and justice with the same tool—the word. The righteous will be blessed with eternal life, and the wicked will be judged (John 5:28-29; Rev 21:1-8).

Evil will be defeated the only way it can be—through non-violent, submissive obedience to God. The book of Revelation speaks of a dragon, symbolizing evil. "But they [Christians] have conquered him [the dragon] by the blood of the Lamb and by the word of their testimony, for they did not cling to life even in the face of death" (Rev 12:11). This gives us a powerful picture of how the death and resurrection of Jesus are still at the center of God's defeat of evil, but now Jesus' followers also join in the victory through giving up their own lives.

Jesus, often depicted in Revelation as the nonviolent Lamb who was killed, was the model and the encouragement for the persecuted Christians of the first century. Today, too, when times get scary and we wonder what we are supposed to do in the face of awful evil, we "follow the Lamb wherever he goes" (Rev 14:4). We live as Jesus lived, through the power of the Spirit.

The church is called to live out the justice and peace of the reign of God right now, anticipating the love and peace of the age to come. We know things aren't perfect and that sin has a lot of power in this world. But through the power of Jesus, the people of God can start living out kingdom values now (Matt 5–7). The church is not the same thing as the kingdom of God, nor can we bring the kingdom of God into its fulfillment on our own strength. But we are witnesses to the kingdom and proof that through Jesus we can do hard things such as sharing our wealth and loving our enemies.

Then I saw a new heaven and a new earth; for the first heaven and the first earth had passed away, and the sea was no more. And I saw the holy city, the new Jerusalem, coming down out of heaven from God. . . .

And I heard a loud voice from the throne saying, "See, the home of God is among mortals. He will dwell with them as their God; they will be his peoples, and God himself will be with them; he will wipe every tear from their eyes. Death will be no more; mourning and crying and pain will be no more, for the first things have passed away."

And the one who was seated on the throne said, "See I am making all things new."

—Revelation 21:1-5

Believers are to be ready. Jesus may come earlier (Matt 24:45-51) or later than we expect (Matt 25:1-13). Jesus tells us clearly that we can't know the hour or day. And we don't have to worry about not knowing this day, because we know what to do to get ready. We serve and follow Jesus in faithful obedience, using our God-given talents (Matt 25:14-30) and caring for those in need (Matt 25:31-46).

The main point of what the Bible says about the end is that God ultimately wins. Following Peter's confession of Jesus as the Christ, Jesus said, "On this rock I will build my church, and the gates of Hades will not prevail against it" (Matt 16:18). God will not abandon the church, whether the Mennonite church or the larger church. God will work through all of us to build the reign of God as we follow Jesus, even if it means sacrifice and suffering. As we follow, we can have joy in knowing we are doing the right thing, the joy of having meaning in our lives, and the joy of being in relationship with the One who loves us best.

A strange and wonderful book

The book of Revelation gives us a series of mysterious pictures of the way the Story ends. To name only a few, we see a throne in heaven surrounded by white-robed people and strange creatures worshiping God (Rev 4); beasts and dragons defeated by a Lamb (Rev 12–14); a dazzling, cube-shaped city, being lowered from heaven (Rev 21). It is more like an abstract painting than a photograph.

While Christians throughout history have tried to use Revelation as a roadmap for end-time events, Revelation's words, like wild paint strokes, are there to help us feel emotion more than give us exact literal details about what will happen. We must remember that this strange conclusion to the Bible was really written as an encouragement for persecuted Christians between AD 90 and 100. These believers needed some reassurance that God would see them through at a time when evil governments seemed to be all-powerful.

The main message of Revelation was for them, and is for us, to follow Jesus and stand firm in our faith, and everything will work out.

Tara: Well? Is this it?

Mary: We went through the Story, so now what?

Luke: The Story is still going on in our lives.

Mike: That is harder to believe, in some ways, than the Israelites' crossing the Red Sea.

Luke: Why?

Mike: It's just hard to imagine that God wants—really wants—to keep doing whatever God is doing . . .

Michele: Building the kingdom?

Mike: Whatever—through someone as ordinary as me.

Rosella: But that is exactly what God wants to do.

Mary: I hear what Mike's saying. I know that's true, but it's hard to comprehend.

Josh: We don't have to be a part of what God is doing. It's a choice.

Mike: Right, and on one level that's absurd. I'm supposed to trust in Something invisible and live differently than the rest of the world because of this invisible Something.

Mary: You can go ahead and say God.

Mike: I'm just trying to be real here. On one level, God asks a lot from people.

Luke: But what's the alternative? Look around you. Even if you had everything, everything you could touch and see, is that all there is to life? Would that really make you satisfied? I don't know about you, but I want more—more than what I see here, more than what money can buy.

Rosella: Here's what I want: I want to live day by day with someone who loves me like nobody else—Jesus. Take everything else away. We are loved, without our deserving it one bit.

Michele: And that is true joy?

Rosella: That is true joy. Even if you suffer, even if your loved ones die—why, there's nothing that can keep us from the love of Christ.

Mike: Yeah. Who wouldn't want that?

The Story continues on

Whether Jesus comes tomorrow or in a thousand years, we live today in the midst of the Story. Isn't that amazing? The Story of Abraham and Sarah, of the 12 disciples, of Mary and Martha, of Paul, Lydia, Timothy, Dorcas, and countless other faithful Christians throughout history—this is our Story, too, if we choose it.

If we choose this Story as our story, everything changes. We choose to believe that there is more to this world than the things we can see and touch. We choose to believe that true joy comes not from money or fame, but from saying yes to God's plan for our lives. We choose to see a different reality shaped by God's Story. We choose Jesus, even as God, long before we were born, chose us.

As we say yes to Jesus and commit ourselves to a dynamic relationship with him, the power of sin is broken. Our relationships are restored. We have a new identity. We are free. We are changed. And we respond in love and gratitude. Our spiritual disciplines and our service to others flow naturally out of who we now are. We find meaning and purpose and joy not out of what we do or how much money we make, but out of who we are in Christ.

This journey is ongoing, full of ups and downs, and maybe raises more questions than we have answers for. But we do not travel alone. We have all of our brothers and sisters in Christ, and we have the Holy Spirit as close to us as our own breath. We love and serve a God who is all-powerful, yet came to us as a baby, a God who is both holy and merciful. We walk and talk with the very Creator of the universe. This journey, this salvation, is completely free and yet costs us everything. It's very hard, yet it's also the most wonderful journey there is.

But we have to choose it. Every one of us is confronted with two basic stories in life. The world says "Live for yourself!" Jesus says, "If any want to become my followers, let them deny themselves and take up their cross daily and follow me. For those who want to save their life will lose it, and those who lose their life for my sake will save it. What does it profit them if they gain the whole world, but lose or forfeit themselves?" (Luke 9:23-25).

Which story will you follow? The way the world has to offer? Or God's way as shown in Jesus? You *will* be part of some story, you *will* take some journey, but whose will it be? How you decide that question affects everything in your life.

The Story waits to become your story. What do you say? What will you do?

Steve Mason/Photodisc/Thinkstock

a **spiritual discipline** to practice:

Draw a timeline of your life. Create some symbols and write a legend for what the symbols mean. For example, if your timeline goes down, it symbolizes a more difficult time in your life; starts mean major turning points; jagged lines mean stress, etc. Try to include every major event in your life to date. This is your story in a drawing (his-story or her-story). Now take time in silence and just listen to what God has to say to you. Then speak to God about each event, both thanking God and asking for a renewed sense of peace and God's presence in your life.

Confession of Faith in a Mennonite Perspective

Article Summary

1. We believe that **God** exists and is pleased with all who draw near by faith. We worship the one holy and loving God who is Father, Son, and Holy Spirit eternally. God has created all things visible and invisible, has brought salvation and new life to humanity through Jesus Christ, and continues to sustain the church and all things until the end of the age.

2. We believe in **Jesus Christ**, the Word of God become flesh. He is the Savior of the world, who has delivered us from the dominion of sin and reconciled us to God by his death on a cross. He was declared to be Son of God by his resurrection from the dead. He is the head of the church, the exalted Lord, the Lamb who was slain, coming again to reign with God in glory.

3. We believe in the **Holy Spirit**, the eternal Spirit of God, who dwelled in Jesus Christ, who empowers the church, who is the source of our life in Christ, and who is poured out on those who believe as the guarantee of redemption.

4. We believe that all **Scripture** is inspired by God through the Holy Spirit for instruction in salvation and training in righteousness. We accept the Scriptures as the Word of God and as the fully reliable and trustworthy standard for Christian faith and life. Led by the Holy Spirit in the church, we interpret Scripture in harmony with Jesus Christ.

The complete articles can be found in *Confession of Faith in a Mennonite Perspective*. Scottdale, PA, and Waterloo, ON: Herald Press, 1995.

5. We believe that God has **created the heavens and the earth** and all that is in them, and that God preserves and renews what has been made. All creation has its source outside itself and belongs to the Creator. The world has been created good because God is good and provides all that is needed for life.

6. We believe that God has **created human beings** in the divine image. God formed them from the dust of the earth and gave them a special dignity among all the works of creation. Human beings have been made for relationship with God, to live in peace with each other, and to take care of the rest of creation.

7. We confess that, beginning with Adam and Eve, humanity has disobeyed God, given way to the tempter, and chosen to **sin**. All have fallen short of the Creator's intent, marred the image of God in which they were created, disrupted order in the world, and limited their love for others. Because of sin, humanity has been given over to the enslaving powers of evil and death.

8. We believe that, through Jesus Christ, God offers **salvation** from sin and a new way of life. We receive God's salvation when we repent and accept Jesus Christ as Savior and Lord. In Christ, we are reconciled with God and brought into the reconciling community. We place our faith in God that, by the same power that raised Christ from the dead, we may be saved from sin to follow Christ and to know the fullness of salvation.

9. We believe that the **church** is the assembly of those who have accepted God's offer of salvation through faith in Jesus Christ. It is the new community of disciples sent into the world to proclaim the reign of God and to provide a foretaste of the church's glorious hope. It is the new society established and sustained by the Holy Spirit.

10. We believe that the **mission** of the church is to proclaim and to be a sign of the kingdom of God. Christ has commissioned the church to make disciples of all nations, baptizing them, and teaching them to observe all things he has commanded.

11. We believe that the **baptism** of believers with water is a sign of their cleansing from sin. Baptism is also a pledge before the church of their covenant with God to walk in the way of Jesus Christ through the power of the Holy Spirit. Believers are baptized into Christ and his body by the Spirit, water, and blood.

12. We believe that the **Lord's Supper** is a sign by which the church thankfully remembers the new covenant which Jesus established by his death. In this communion meal, the church renews its covenant with God and with each other and participates in the life and death of Jesus Christ until he comes.

13. We believe that in **washing the feet** of his disciples, Jesus calls us to serve one another in love as he did. Thus, we acknowledge our frequent need of cleansing, renew our willingness to let go of pride and worldly power, and offer our lives in humble service and sacrificial love.

14. We practice **discipline** in the church as a sign of God's offer of transforming grace. Discipline is intended to liberate erring brothers and sisters from sin and to restore them to a right relationship with God and to fellowship in the church. The practice of discipline gives integrity to the church's witness in the world.

15. We believe that **ministry** is a continuation of the work of Christ, who gives gifts through the Holy Spirit to all believers and empowers them for service in the church and in the world. We also believe that God calls particular persons in the church to specific leadership ministries and offices. All who minister are accountable to God and to the community of faith.

16. We believe that the church of Jesus Christ is **one body** with many members, ordered in such a way that, through the one Spirit, believers may be built together spiritually into a dwelling place for God.

17. We believe that Jesus Christ calls us to **discipleship**, to take up our cross and follow him. Through the gift of God's saving grace, we are empowered to be disciples of Jesus, filled with his Spirit, following his teachings and his path through suffering to new life. As we are faithful to his way, we become conformed to Christ and separated from the evil in the world.

18. We believe that to be a disciple of Jesus is to know **life in the Spirit**. As the life, death, and resurrection of Jesus Christ takes shape in us, we grow in the image of Christ and in our relationship with God. The Holy Spirit is active in individual and in communal worship, leading us deeper into the experience of God.

19. We believe that God intends human life to begin in **families** and to be blessed through families. Even more, God desires all people to become part of the church, God's family. As single and married members of the church family give and receive nurture and healing, families can grow toward the wholeness that God intends. We are called to chastity and to loving faithfulness in marriage.

20. We commit ourselves to tell the **truth**, to give a simple yes or no, and to avoid the swearing of oaths.

21. We believe that everything belongs to God, who calls the church to live in faithful **stewardship** of all that God has entrusted to us and to participate now in the rest and justice which God has promised.

22. We believe that **peace** is the will of God. God created the world in peace, and God's peace is most fully revealed in Jesus Christ, who is our peace and the peace of the whole world. Led by the Holy Spirit, we follow Christ in the way of peace, doing justice, bringing reconciliation, and practicing nonresistance, even in the face of violence and warfare.

23. We believe that the church is God's holy nation, called to give full allegiance to Christ its head and to witness to every **nation, government, and society** about God's saving love.

24. We place our hope in the **reign of God** and its fulfillment in the day when Christ will come again in glory to judge the living and the dead. He will gather his church, which is already living under the reign of God. We await God's final victory, the end of this present age of struggle, the resurrection of the dead, and a new heaven and a new earth. There the people of God will reign with Christ in justice, righteousness, and peace for ever and ever.

Resources for Further Study

Mennonite Identity and Thought

Claim(ing) Faith: Youth Discover the Confession of Faith. Harrisonburg, VA, and Waterloo, ON: MennoMedia, 2013. Designed to introduce youth to the *Confession of Faith in a Mennonite Perspective*. Includes activities and discussion-starters.

Confession of Faith in a Mennonite Perspective. Scottdale, PA, and Waterloo, ON: Herald Press, 1995. This confession, used by Mennonite Church Canada and Mennonite Church USA, gives a succinct overview of Anabaptist theology. *God's Story, Our Story* is grounded in this understanding of Christian faith.

Murray, Stuart. *The Naked Anabaptist: The Bare Essentials of a Radical Faith*. Scottdale, PA , and Waterloo, ON: Herald Press, 2010. A book that catches a vision for living a life of radical faith.

Nolt, Steve. *Through Fire and Water: An Overview of Mennonite History*, rev. ed. Scottdale, PA, and Waterloo, ON: Herald Press, 2010. A very readable book of Anabaptist history geared for high school readers. It presents the story in the scope of church history.

The Radicals. 1999. A dramatic story on DVD about the early Anabaptists, illustrating the commitments necessary to be part of the faith story.

Roth, John. *Beliefs: Mennonite Faith and Practice*. Scottdale, PA , and Waterloo, ON: Herald Press, 2004. An easy-to-read book that provides interpretations for beliefs and faithful discipleship in the Mennonite Church.

_____. *Practices: Mennonite Worship and Witness*. Scottdale, PA, and Waterloo, ON: Herald Press, 2009. Examines Mennonite worship and practice.

_____. *Stories: How Mennonites Came to Be*. Scottdale, PA, and Waterloo, ON: Herald Press, 2006. An engaging account of the Mennonite story.

Snyder, C. Arnold. *Anabaptist History and Theology: An Introduction*. Kitchener, ON: Pandora Press, 1995. An excellent resource for Anabaptist history.

Who Are the Mennonites? Harrisonburg, VA: Third Way Media, 2010. A DVD that explores Mennonite history, beliefs, and practices in an understandable way.

Life of Jesus

Blosser, Don, Timothy J. Dailey, Randy Petersen, and Dietrich Gruen. *Jesus: His Life and Times*. Lincolnwood, IL: Publications International, 1999. An easy-reading summary of the life of Christ. It also connects the life of Jesus to the entire biblical story of God's people and gives the reader a good background to the history and culture of Jesus' day.

Kraybill, Donald. *The Upside-Down Kingdom*, updated ed. Harrisonburg, VA, and Waterloo, ON: Herald Press, 2011. A good book about peace and many other aspects of the Christian life.

Yancey, Philip. *The Jesus I Never Knew*. Grand Rapids, MI: Zondervan Publishing, 1995. A good read on the cultural world of Jesus. Yancey also helps articulate the interpretation issues, using the Sermon on the Mount as an example.

Yoder, John Howard. *The Politics of Jesus*. Grand Rapids, MI: Eerdmans Publishing, 1972. While the book is an excellent read for academic scholarship in general, for our purposes, it can be used to discuss Old Testament Jubilee understandings.

Spiritual Disciplines

The 24/7 Experience: A DVD Curriculum on Following Jesus Every Day. Grand Rapids, MI: Zondervan, 2006. A resource that documents youth traveling around the U.S. to meet with Jesus-followers who are making a difference in their world. Includes discussion questions.

Augsburger, David W. *Helping People Forgive*. Louisville, KY: Westminster John Knox Press, 1996. A great resource for understanding biblical forgiveness and how it applies to our lives.

Bass, Dorothy, and Don Richter, eds. *Way to Live: Christian Practices for Teens*. Nashville, TN: The Upper Room, 2002. Each chapter is written by a young person and an adult and provides spiritual practices for everyday life and putting faith into action.

Boers, Arthur. *Day by Day These Things We Pray: Uncovering Ancient Rhythms of Prayer*. Scottdale, PA, and Waterloo, ON: Herald Press, 2010. Invites us to claim the practice of prayer and grow our relationship with God.

Breeze, Cindy Massanari. *Dive: Devotions for Deeper Living*. Harrisonburg, VA, and Waterloo, ON: Herald Press, 2012. A devotional book for youth, grounded in Scripture and prayer.

Foster, Richard J. *Celebration of Discipline: The Path to Spiritual Growth*. San Francisco: HarperSanFrancisco, 1988. Provides a concise but thorough summary of the disciplines.

Hershberger, Michele. *A Christian View of Hospitality: Expecting Surprises*. Scottdale, PA, and Waterloo, ON: Herald Press, 1999. While not a book on spiritual disciplines per se, it does articulate the disciplines as part of a whole life change. Hospitality is not ultimately something you do. It's something you are. That is true of all disciplines.

McKnight, Scott, Chris Folmsbee, and Sylar Thomas. *The Jesus Creed for Students: Loving God, Loving Others*. Brewster, MA: Paraclete Press, 2011. Explores what it means to love God and love others.

Thompson, Marjorie J. *Soul Feast: An Invitation to the Christian Spiritual Life*. Louisville, KY: Westminster John Knox Press, 1995. A beautifully written summary of eight spiritual disciplines. Thompson does a great job of helping the reader negotiate through the temptations of legalism and forcing God's blessing.

White, Julie Ellison. *Tent of Meeting: A 25-Day Adventure with God*. Scottdale, PA, and Waterloo, ON: Faith and Life Resources, 2004. A journal that helps youth grow spiritually through the practice of spiritual disciplines.

Yaconelli, Mark. *Downtime: Helping Teenagers Pray*. Grand Rapids, MI: Zondervan, 2008. Provides tools to help you guide youth in a life of prayer. Includes prayer exercises and explores classical and more recent forms of prayer.

Yamasaki, April. *Sacred Pauses*. Harrisonburg, VA, and Waterloo, ON: Herald Press, 2013. An introduction to spiritual practices in the everyday, allowing our lives to be centered on God.

Especially for Youth Leaders

Brubacher Kaethler, Andy, and Bob Yoder, eds. *Youth Ministry at a Crossroads: Tending to the Faith Formation of Mennonite Youth*. Harrisonburg, VA, and Waterloo, ON: Herald Press, 2011. Writers provide insight and encouragement for faith formation in youth and explore contexts where formation happens.

Clark, Chap. *Hurt 2.0: Inside the World of Today's Teenagers*. Grand Rapids, MI: Baker Academic, 2011. An update of the original best-seller, *Hurt*, this book includes new research, statistics, and documentation. It provides an open look at the experiences of today's youth and the issues they face.

Dean, Kenda Creasy. *Almost Christian: What the Faith of Our Teenagers Is Telling the American Church*. New York: Oxford University Press, 2010. Explores youth attitudes toward Christianity and faith practice and is urgent in the need to create a "consequential faith."

Powell, Kara, and Chap Clark. *Sticky Faith: Everyday Ideas to Build Lasting Faith in Youth*. Grand Rapids, MI: Zondervan, 2011. Based on Fuller Youth Institute findings, the book presents ways to actively encourage spiritual growth in young people. Also available as a teen curriculum with DVD.

Timeline

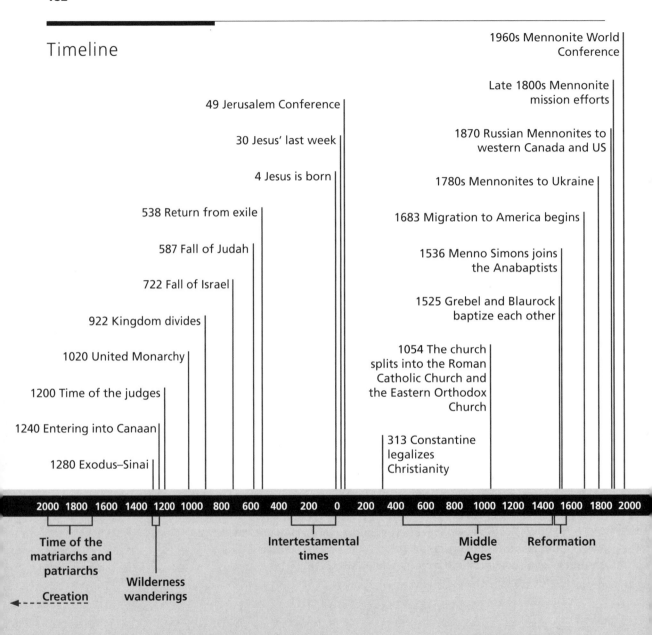

1960s Mennonite World Conference

Late 1800s Mennonite mission efforts

49 Jerusalem Conference

1870 Russian Mennonites to western Canada and US

30 Jesus' last week

4 Jesus is born

1780s Mennonites to Ukraine

538 Return from exile

1683 Migration to America begins

587 Fall of Judah

1536 Menno Simons joins the Anabaptists

722 Fall of Israel

1525 Grebel and Blaurock baptize each other

922 Kingdom divides

1020 United Monarchy

1054 The church splits into the Roman Catholic Church and the Eastern Orthodox Church

1200 Time of the judges

1240 Entering into Canaan

313 Constantine legalizes Christianity

1280 Exodus–Sinai

| 2000 | 1800 | 1600 | 1400 | 1200 | 1000 | 800 | 600 | 400 | 200 | 0 | 200 | 400 | 600 | 800 | 1000 | 1200 | 1400 | 1600 | 1800 | 2000 |

Time of the matriarchs and patriarchs

Intertestamental times

Middle Ages

Reformation

Creation

Wilderness wanderings

The Author

Michele Hershberger teaches youth ministry and Bible at Hesston (Kan.) College. A popular youth speaker in the Mennonite Church and beyond, she is also author of five curricula and two books, including *A Christian View of Hospitality: Expecting Surprises* (Herald Press), and *What Gives: Using God's Money* (Faith & Life Resources), and *Now It Springs Up*, co-authored with Carol Duerksen and Laurie Oswald Robinson. She and her husband Del live in Hesston and have three children.